Tales From The Punkside – An Anthology

Sothira Pheng – Crucifix – by Jacky Smith

Co-edited by Gregory Bull and Mike Dines

Itchy Monkey Press

www.talesfromthepunkside.com

All work copyright to the original author or artist 2014

Front and Back Cover Design and layout by Greg Bull

Printed in the UK by Lulu

No part of this publication may be reproduced, stored in or introduced into a retrieval system, or transmitted, in any form or by any means (electronic, mechanical, photocopying, recording or otherwise), without the prior written permission of the copyright owner, except by a reviewer who may quote brief passages in a review.

This book is sold subject to the condition that it shall not, by way of trade or otherwise, be lent, re-sold, hired out or otherwise circulated without the author's prior consent in any form of binding or cover other than that in which it is published and without a similar condition including this condition being imposed on the subsequent purchaser.

Published by Itchy Monkey Press 2014

Gregory Bull would like to dedicate this anthology to the unmentioned heroes of the peace punk movement – the pamphleteers, the poster artists, the squatters, the young punks who put gigs on in the local village hall and finally the punks who paid out their "no more than" £1.50 to get into a gig.

Mike Dines would like to dedicate this book to those who have shared their tales and punk-inspired tribulations with him over the years - to Kev the punk, Steve Maxted, Reeta, Nafe and Sam (my lovely wife); to those who have told their many tales to many people across the globe, in faraway corners of faraway places - at gigs, pubs and squats; and finally to those who continue to inspire future tales from the punkside - and the future generations of subversives, oiks and reprobates. The sharing of adventures, experiences and stories are what connects us all. Thanks.

If you find any artwork in this book which was created by yourself and you wish it to be removed or you would like to be credited please contact gregorybull1@gmail.com

CONTENTS

Glue and Bastards Alastair Gordon — 12

Everyone Was an Anarchist Alistair Livingstone — 20

Golden Brown Market Amanda Bigler — 28

The Outcasts: Punk in Northern Ireland during the troubles Francis Stewart — 33

A Flower in the Desert Greg Bull — 46

The Political Pioneers of Punk (just don't mention the f-word!) Helen Reddington — 50

IT WAS WHAT IT WAS… "Es delito ser Punk" Isobel Flores — 72

Disgustin' Justin Justine Butler — 82

Poetry Pieces Laura Way — 87

DUNSTAN BRUCE, AND WHY IS HISTORY SO UP FOR ANARCHO-PUNK? Lucy Robinson — 90

Bottom-feeding on the Crusty Carousel Martin Cooper — 98

They May Have Beds, but They Don't Use Sheets Rebecca Binns — 104

Crusty Robert Dellar — 115

Not Just Boys' Fun (with apologies to 7 Seconds) Sarah Attfield — 126

You Can Live Forever In Paradise On Earth Ted Curtis — 140

Introduction

I first heard the term 'anarcho-narrative' from a close friend of mine who, incidentally is not, was not, and probably never will be, a punk. It was not the actual concept that had drawn his attention, but rather the term 'anarcho': he knew that I had an interest in anarcho-punk and therefore jumped on the anarchistic leanings of this story-telling endeavour. Excited, he told me of this 'unbook' being published by two academic librarians, Andrew Walsh and Emma Coonan, a project concerned with what they saw as the linking of a 'series of narratives connected by the overarching theme of information discovery journeys'[1]. The remit was deliberately broad, allowing authors to be free to decide the appropriate structure of their submissions, as well as the format. Indeed, both editors encouraged budding writers to move away from more traditional contexts, instead promoting the use of poetry, transcripts of social media, illustrative fictional prose, or 'whatever media seems appropriate to the author'.[2]

Although I found it a bit odd to see the term 'anarcho' in this context, the organic nature of the project grabbed my attention. Authors were empowered to write in their own style, with very little interference from the editors. 'We hope the anarchical strand running throughout it manages to stand out', writes Coonan and Walsh, 'using anarchy to mean the lowest possible level of organization, such as suits the reader or author rather than the editors or publisher. Although the print format imposes an element of central rule upon the book we've tried to make it as easy to break out of as possible'.[3] And it was the emphasis on these two areas - the experimental freedom offered to the authors, and minimal editorial constraint - that drew me towards the publishing of my own project. Ideas began to form in my mind. What about the telling of everyday punk narratives by those who were there? How about asking writers to convey – through prose, poetry, art – the experiences that many had had but were never written down, like the squatting, the drinking, the glue sniffing? What about writing about being a provincial punk; of starting up your own punk band (that lasted for 3 months); or of missing your favourite band play live because your mum wouldn't let you go out 'looking like that?' Perhaps I could provide a space for those punks to tell their own story? To write, in whatever context they felt comfortable, about their own experiences of punk?

At the same time as I was bringing the anarcho-narrative project to life, I was also involved in editing an academic work dealing with the anarcho-punk scene of the 1980s. I had sent out a 'call for chapters' - very much like I had done for Tales From the Punkside[4] - but this time in a more 'academic' manner, and was getting ready to sort through proposals, putting together those submissions that

---

[1] http://librarywriting.blogspot.co.uk/2013/01/call-for-chapters-anarcho-narrative.html. The book itself, *Only Connect...discovery pathways, library explorations, and the information adventure* (2013) can be found at http://innovativelibraries.org.uk/index.php/onlyconnect/
[2] http://librarywriting.blogspot.co.uk/2013/01/call-for-chapters-anarcho-narrative.html
[3] http://innovativelibraries.org.uk/index.php/onlyconnect/

[4] A 'call for papers' is a process whereby an editor send out an invitation via internet mailing lists asking writers if they would like to contribute to a book.

would make a good academic volume. Afterwards I was to email those whose submissions were 'successful', outlining specific word-count, what style of font they should use (and of course what size), what referencing each author should use and what kind of date we are looking to receive first drafts. After reading and editing these first drafts I was to return them to the author for them to make necessary changes, and ask them to submit again at another deadline. Then, with a final reading, the volume would be sent off to an academic publisher, and the process would start all over again. Although necessary, this process seemed to detract from the subject matter somewhat, indeed adding further to the abstract stance of each chapter. Ideas had to be backed up by academic texts, for instance, and methodology had to be deconstructed. And words such as, say 'deconstructed', had to be used to give the volume a sense of academicism.

I am certainly not condemning the academic process, I am after all an 'academic', but it seemed to me that the academic rigour of editing and submitting in this way somehow diluted the very essence of the subject matter we were dealing with. In fact, subject matter was almost relegated to second place behind academic hierarchies; of 'I know more than you do' debates and doctoral fisty-cuffs behind the bike-sheds after school. And so, I decided to do something different. The academics would often have their say, but what about the many tales that I have heard from my punk friends and peer group, the many mischievous shenanigans that so many of my cohort had 'got up to', and the many scrapes and near-misses that these individuals had encountered? Where was the everyday, the 'normal' in these academic accounts? If academicism was sometimes more concerned with theories and long words than deciphering the day-by-day comings and goings of those who defined themselves as 'punk', what about the individuals who felt no need to apply convoluted academic theories or debates to justify subcultural membership? It almost feels as if the academic has to encroach on the everyday, not allowing these tales any autonomy; to not let them sit on their own, for what they are, without interpretation or analysis.

Yet, if I wanted to move away from the academic side of writing and editing, I also wanted to acknowledge other influences that made a real impact on me as I was growing up as a young punk. As well as annoying the hell out of my mum by playing Extreme Noise Terror at full blast, I also loved reading books that were deemed 'punk fiction', such as Gobbing, Pogoing and Gratuitous Bad Language (1996), an anthology of punk short stories edited by Robert Dellar, Seaton Point (1998), a novel written by seven authors (Robert Dellar, Ted Curtis, Martin Cooper, Rob Colson, Lucy Williams, Mally Mallinson and Emma McElwee) and Simon Strong's A259 Multiplex Bomb Outrage (1995). These books, alongside the writings of Stewart Home and the poetry of Andy T portrayed a punk scene that seemed, ironically, more 'real', even though they were often classed as fiction, and in many ways blurred the difference between fiction and memoir. Indeed, it is great to see two recent publications – Ted Curtis' The Darkening Light (2014) and Robert Dellar's memoir Splitting in Two: Mad Pride and Punk Rock Oblivion (2014) – continue in this vein.

As I write, I also realize a major flaw in my argument. After all, I'm critiquing academia for doing something that is, by its very nature what it is: the critical enquiry into ideas. And indeed, this type of debate has been raging in academic circles for a long time, since the publication of the Centre for Contemporary Cultural Studies' Resistance Through Rituals: Youth Subcultures in Post-War Britain

(1976) and Dick Hedige's Subculture: The Meaning of Style in 1979. Nor am I saying that all academic writing is bad. Quite the opposite. I suppose, I'm just saying, that's all. I suppose I want that which I cannot have: a non-academic, non-judgmental piece of punk writing that just says something for its own sake, with no axe to grind, no theoretical position to defend and no need for a meet behind the bike sheds. I know it ain't gonna happen, but it's worth a try, hey?

I am not saying that I have achieved this within Tales From the Punkside. Indeed, I'm not even sure if I have reproduced the 'anarcho-narrative' nature of the project as seen in the volume published by Walsh and Coonan. But hey, I'm not too worried about that to be honest. Instead, it has just been fantastic to read the tales of those who were 'there'; those whose stories are not 'important' enough to sit alongside the memoirs of the punk rock 'jet set'. I wanted to read stories of what it was like to squat in London in the 1980s, what it was like to live as a provincial punk. I wanted to read of the darkness of glue sniffing and to hear the memoirs of punk in other countries. In other words, to hear from the silent majority, those who did not have a chance to tell their tales of their punkside.

Although this book began in a rainy afternoon as an excited friend told me he'd seen that 'A' word, I would not have been able to complete it without the following people. Obviously I would really like to thank Greg Bull: his help in pulling the final project together at a time when work constraints were beginning to kick in was invaluable. Greg stepped in as a fantastic editor and project manager whilst I was stuck on a train to and from London. I would also like to say thanks to all of those who backed this project – obviously without their financial help it would have been far more difficult to get a print run – and hopefully another cash injection that will allow Itchy Monkey Press to continue. Thanks so much to you all – and I hope you like the book! A big thank-you to those who have contributed to the book and for giving up their time to tell us their tales of their punkside: each one as valuable as the next in terms of narrating personal experiences of punk. Thanks also to Alistair Livingstone, Lucy Robinson and Dunstan Bruce for allowing us to use their work, to Jon Leftley, Alastair Gordon and Matt Worley for their thoughts and Emma Coonan and Andrew Walsh for allowing me to swipe their idea. Last, but not least, I would also like to say thanks to Sam, Eric, Spike and Molly for inspiration. I hope you all enjoy the book!

Mike Dines – Summer 2014

A Very Special Thank You goes out to all these people who pledged enough money to make this publication a reality.

Thank you. Greg and Mike

Helena Adams	Paul Gluba
Katie B	Tommaso Gravante
Jon Beetham	Matt Grimes
Claire Bone	Louise Jackson
Greg Bull	Alice LaPoma
Rich Cross	Alistair Livingstone
Derry Curry	Kirsty Lohman
Ted Curtis	Luke Scott
Alan Dines	Bengi-Sue Sirin
Sandra Dines	Francis Stewart
Thomas DeHart	Joe Townsend
Kevin Dunn	Andrew Walsh
Colin Fergusson	Laura Way
Chloe Francis	Matt Worley
Jessica Gluba	

Foreword

I wasn't a card-carrying anarchist. I probably only considered myself a "punk" for about 6 months. I was dressing in all sorts of styles during my years as a sixteen, seventeen, eighteen, etc year old back in 1981,82 and 83. Never happy to stay with one style for long. Able to fit in with whatever gig I was at. Or able to make sure I didn't look the same as the rest. This freedom gave me a sense of perspective, even at the time, of being an observer more than a being actually taking part in what was going on around me. Content to live a safe domestic life watching the TV. Watching the football. Just being alive. And observing.

One day I decided to spike my hair up into huge spikes like Cal from Discharge, put on an old black dinner jacket, black ripped jeans and huge army boots. I paraded through town feeling like a peacock. Everyone stared. The spikes must have been about 10 inches long. I went for a piss in the loos in a well-known department store and as I stood there pissing about 4 or 5 black guys came in and just stared at me. I thought my time was up. Really. One of them asked me "Why you dress up like that?" and I replied [bravely for me], "Because I like it. And because I can". The questioner looked at his mates then turned back to me with a smile and said, "Your foolish man. But it's cool". They then turned and left laughing to each other. I felt on top of the world. Other times you would get chased and occasionally thumped and have beer thrown at you in pubs [or worse]. But it was great to be young. Even back then I knew it wasn't going to last. But luckily I never managed to grow up properly.

I spent a lot of times at punk and peace punk gigs just observing what was going on around me. Quite often I spent the entire time during a band set on my own. Observing. And I would try and take what good things came out of the music and the political statements.

I loved the message of Crass and Discharge but at the time would be more likely to be listening to Joy Division or Magazine. I found a lot of the punk music uninteresting. Especially on record. But live… that was another matter. And reading those fold out black and white singles with "Pay No More Than" on the front. That was my political education.

This was the time of Margaret Thatcher, the Miners' Strike and the growth of mass-media and selfishness. The peace punks and anarchists revolted against that and tried to Stop The City. There was something to fight against.

This collection gives us an insight into the times through prose, poetry, recollections, short stories and academic reflections.

I found myself as co-editor of this project by accident but it has been a great pleasure to read the submissions and get it all together in one volume.

We hope you enjoy this eclectic mix of material.

Greg Bull – Summer 2014

Gig Flyer by Persons Unknown

Glue and Bastards *Alastair Gordon*

Round Hill primary school field, Beeston, Nottinghamshire. Circa March 1981. This was a small town suffering the early effects of Thatcherite policy. Youth unemployment was skyrocketing and the chances of getting a job of any description were slack for my generation. The echoes of the Sex Pistols 'No Future' mantra was a steady fixture of my thinking back then. All the government offered to the rising crises in unemployment was to put my generation on youth opportunities schemes Youth Opportunities, the Youth Training Schemes....this was the future to look forward to. I poured the Zoff, plaster remover onto my red and black jumper sleeve and took a big suck. The icy taste filled my mouth. The hit was almost instant. The sense of reality my thirteen year old body was annihilated in a moment. Echoes filled my head, together with a sense of euphoria. Balance was clearly lost and a fuzzy, warm feeling covered my body. The hot summer day took on a new sense of reality; a new consciousness that would become increasingly familiar over the next few years. The grass under my feet felt unstable, balance was lost. Waves of disorientation undulated and swarmed through my head and an uncontrollable laughter burst out. Pleasure had been discovered for this young punk. I woke up after what seemed like a very deep sleep. Thinking I'd been out for hours it turned out I'd only been high for a few minutes. This was the pattern of sniffing various substances containing the dangerous chemicals that proved socially addictive.

Sniffing glue was popular within and without the punk scene in Beeston and throughout the UK. Tabloids screamed headlines of death and danger stemming from this new youth craze. From 1977 onwards I'd fallen in love with punk rock. The title of the zine, *Sniffing Glue* would not be discovered by this young punk for some time. All I knew was that it was dangerous, parents were scared and outraged by this practice and that was enough for me. Memory fails me how I came to be on the school field or who had the magical substance that day. Suffice to say the effects of that short sniff were to populate my life for some time. The industrial town of Beeston was in decline and ravaged by the Thatcherite policies of deindustrialisation. Unemployment was high and all the school I attended had in store for us was to be sent to the local factory once we'd left with next to nothing in terms of qualifications. Not that I cared, my education flew out of the stereo speakers from bands like Crass, UK Subs and Discharge. That music made clear sense to me (still does now). The scene in the early eighties was populated, predictably by a number of factions and these were in school. The group of friends I was with in 1981 changed frequently during this time, the original group of punks I associated were mostly into UK82 punk like the Exploited, Chron Gen and Blitz, much drawn from the legacy of the Sex Pistols (Glasper, 2004). I was a paper boy working at a number of newshops in the town. Journeying on my rounds I often encountered the odd discarded gluebag. Such items were strange, dried up affairs, often resembling a weird cast –off from some dubious sexual practice: a giant, used condom. As teenagers inevitably explore the nooks and crannies of their hometown environments, numerous examples of these bags could be discovered in graveyards, surrounding electricity substations and recreation parks. What often accompanied these relics were discarded rolled up tubes and tins of Evo Stick adhesive, soggy old boxes of freezer bags and cigarette butts. It was clear a thriving subculture surrounding this was evident in the town. The question that bugged me was who was responsible?

School was shit for me. I could not stand it, not only did I suffer from extreme, social anxiety, the teachers, for the most part were a bunch of prats. I loved to read books, loved music and writing, though the school experience never acted as a creative catalyst for me. My love of history was soured on a weekly basis by an awful authoritarian teacher. One particular afternoon when the class was trawling through the finer, uncritical points of Richard III and the children in the tower, a rather interesting character that had been expelled from the school came into the classroom. Bleached, spiky red hair, a filthy bootleg Westwood 'Destroy' cheesecloth and forearm tattoos: a rather impressive Peter and The Test-tube Babies 'Up Yer Bum' design. There was something else to this character. He slurred out, "can you sign this form, Sir", arms hanging listlessly, the red hair making his complexion pasty, punctuated by copious chin spots and unusually red lips. Richard III was handsome by comparison. He was the best anti role-model I'd seen for some time out of his head and 100% punk. On the way home from school later the glue bags on the path we walked in-between the golf course were visible. The trademark of the unknown pleasure was evident

Rumours circulated around various peer groups that a few of the punks in the final year were into glue sniffing. These people compared to us third year novice punks were seriously cool. Always wearing the right UK82 clothes and displaying an impeccable disregard for authority of any type. They were seen frequently in and around the home town often boarding buses to hang out with other punks in Nottingham's Market Square. It was inevitable one of us was going to try this sooner or later...it was only a matter of time. My punk peer groups fluctuated during this period as the trial and error of finding good friends led me down a few cul-de-sacs. One of the staple themes of young teen discussion was glue sniffing. The Zoff incident above was the first time I'd been high or inebriated. It opened a new world up to me. That said it was not the real deal. Evo Stick was. This required freezer bags and the said solvent ensuring the correct high could be secured.

The paper round I had provided the income to purchase the first tubes of glue. The first time I tried sniffing was a solitary affair. The local Woolworths on the high street sold the glue. One summer afternoon in 1981 I purchased a tube of the red beast from Woolworths for twenty-five pence together with two packets of polo mints to mask the solvent smell. The bags were lifted from the cupboard at home. Some of the land at the end of my street was being redeveloped and housing built there. After the paper round I cycled up there ensconcing myself in the dusty first floor of the new build, surrounded by bags of cement and the aroma of fresh plaster. Summer was in full swing, the sound of children playing down the street added to the sense of personal change. It wasn't that long since I would have been playing down with them on my bike. Now I had a new potential hobby. With my bike safely stashed around the back of this house, I began my journey. The tube of glue had a tiny aluminium nipple that had to be broken off. The pungent odour of the glue instantly evident. Squirting half of this into the corner of the freezer bag, the top was folded over my hand. This technique I had observed from a lone punk staggering down Chilwell High Road some weeks earlier, with him blowing into the bag and breathing the fumes back in by pushing and squeezing the bag. Sat there in my little hideaway I began to do the same. The taste differed from the Zoff yet the high was 100% more powerful than this, instant and brutal. The taste as the vapours rose was oddly sweet. The bag began to echo, the more I breathed in the more the definition of vision began to blur. Echoes governed my hearing, auditory hallucinations of the first order. Thoughts became pleasurable in their confusion as unknown music began to fill my head in time with the rhythm of the bag. The high became deeper as the evening sounds and light collapsed into dreams.

Retrospectively it's difficult to recall what happened next, consciousness shut down though. I remembered nothing of the session awaking some hours later in the same room, covered in cement and plaster dust. This was hardly the most promising of starts to the new high, though for some particular reason the opening few minutes were amazing, indescribable really. Something told me it would not be the last time I'd be doing this.

My dad took a job in Dhahran, Saudi Arabia early in 1980 to stave off the looming unemployment crisis and free him from a failing marriage and dead-end job managing the local council depot. As a result he was absent for six month or longer periods. The result was I had the chance to run pretty much free, choosing to mostly ignore any authority my mother and brother feebly tried to foist upon me. The house we lived in was on the same street from my new found glue den. It took some time to gather myself together whilst constructing a believable excuse about what I'd been up to. Polo mints were devoured at a rapid rate in a feeble attempt to disguise the overpowering odour of glue, the crunch echoing through my newly addled head. The skin around my mouth felt delicate as if a rash was due to set in. My hands had glue residue, turning black from all the dust I'd been rolling around in my glued up state. Most of this was easy to remove but there were always little telltale spots that I would spot over the forthcoming days. I got in and remember my mum looking strange, I don't think she noticed but I still felt out of it, feeling paranoid that I felt sure she'd notice the smell. My 'get out of jail' story was already prepared: I would have said I'd been gluing the seat on my bike which had a split...., the perfect excuse. I remember that night feeling elated. I'd got away with my first glue-sniffing venture and was ready for the next day at school.

The next day's paper round was completed in a groggy manner and I felt sure I'd made a few mistakes. Sod it. At least I made it round. The walk up the golf-course path to school with various mates was as per usual and I kept tight lipped about the sniffing episode, that was my secret for now. Lessons and assembly for me were of the usual disinteresting CSE diet of boredom. Most of my time in lessons was consumed either by daydreaming or causing disruption acting the goat with the other never do wells of the class. Ten o'clock was breaktime, marked with the usual spilling out of the rowdy pupils. This was also the time for the smokers to gather at the appointed place on the school field, safe from the prying eyes of the teachers supervising the usual chaos. Two of the smokers crowd were brothers a year or so above me, John and Pete. Both were adopted and had been in trouble for various offenses at the school and beyond. Neither were punks but I knew that John was into sniffing for sure. Quietly I told him about my previous nights exploits and asked if he fancied going sniffing later in the week. The answer was of course, yes, as agreed we'd meet after the paper rounds in the high road at five. Friday was payday so I was covered to get more glue.

The school week dragged in the same way the week began. I hated school and never felt it challenged me or allowed creativity. To me it was more often than not about following rules and adhering to a hidden curriculum: I made it my mission to secretly fuck with the rules at every opportunity. No one in our year was fooled by rosy career talks for the religious freak of a deputy headmaster; we knew there was massive youth unemployment. Sniffing was a clear escape from this pressure. We all knew we'd either be on the dole or stuck on a shitty scheme in a couple of years. Friday arrived and I was excited, the last glue buzz was marred by oblivion, this time I felt sure some of the hallucinations I'd overhead in playground discussions would visit me, well hopefully. All was not going to go to plan.

It was the tail end of a scorching hot summer's day in Beeston and, as usual I called into Woolworths for a Slush Puppy, and this time I'd get two tubes of Evo Stick. I was pretty well paid in those days for the paper round and also did the Sunday morning shift which paid over a pound for the session. The till girl didn't bat an eyelid at the two tubes of glue, this was the time before the major local panic fired by the *Nottingham Evening Post* about the 'lethal youth craze' of sniffing had took hold.

I met John at the end of the high road, he was on foot and we walked back up to my house to drop my bike off. We headed to the golf course; I'd managed to stuff a few freezer bags into my jeans pocket. The usual pisstaking and horseplay happened while we made our way to the golf-course. John was a fair bit taller than me and pretty handy in a fight. He was always in trouble for one thing or another and always managed to slip away leaving someone else with the blame, pretty clever. Equally, there was an uncanny, disordered sense to his general persona. While he wasn't a punk and always banging on about Dexys Midnight Runners who I thought were shite we got on pretty well. I'd met him as part of garden creeping and general trouble causing gang. We'd ride around on bikes firing berries with catapults at suburban windows, annoy the super rich on Beeston Fields Drive by ringing doorbells and running off and lots of similar, typical teenage behaviour. By far the Garden creeping was the most fun. There was one rule. You had to get from one end of a street to another by climbing over fences and not being discovered. Inevitably we were often chased by angry householders and occasionally the police. We always managed to get away, meeting up afterwards in fits of laughter. That said the fearlessness of John always gave the impression of him being slightly disturbed. He never discussed his past and all I knew of him was he and his brother lived with his stepparents. His stepmother was terminally ill.

Even in this summer weather John wore a donkey jacket, jeans and dockers. I never saw him dress any different. I had my usual regulation red and black striped jumper on, black bondage trousers and dockers. We got the entrance of the golf course. We had to be careful. Aside from the path through the middle this was a private playground of the rich. Frequent signs warned of trespassers being prosecuted: they were there to be ignored. All the local kids ignored this and the woods surrounding the golf course were a regular haunt of local kids who built dens, played hide and seek and got up to general mischief. One of the main 'hobbies' was collecting the lost golf balls and selling them on to Bowden's second hand shop on Chilwell road for ten pence a pop. This time we were on a different mission. Once the coast was clear of golfers crossing from one course to another, we snuck in. John knew the way, and we darted down a long path surrounded by tall trees and bushes. At the end of the path, a disused swimming pool greeted us. The summer heat had dried the remaining water to a small muddy puddle at one end. We sat on the side, John said no one ever came through here, we were safe. We sparked up a Benson and Hedges cigarettes down to the nubs from a ten pack, passing the time for a bit in the early evening sunshine sat on the side of the pool. Each of us had a gob puddle forming, each bit of spit punctuating the conversation with the occasional 'fizz' of the ash as it landed on the mess. Eventually with a couple of fag nubs sizzling in the gob puddles we got the freezer bags out. I handed John the red tube of Evo, he said he'd pay me back on Monday at school. Caps broke off and fresh glue in the bags we began to sniff. The familiar pungent flavour filled my mouth, the warm, crackly feeling echoing across my body and into my head. The last time I sniffed I took it easy with the glue. John saw it differently as a seasoned sniffer. We'd got into it, the usual antics occurred, running and staggering from one end of the pool. We were having a right laugh, my thoughts were jumbled up, the colours of the world became much brighter, the rushes from the glue getting much stronger. Nothing could top this, we felt unbeatable. Then it began to go wrong.

We were shitfaced; John produced a new half tin of glue from his pocket. The two earlier bags were now dried up, early dusk was closing in and the golfers were turning into the clubhouse in the fading light. I was really out of it and felt a bit scared, I didn't want to get more smashed but agreed. The metal seal of the glue tin was punctured in with John's house key. This time he poured loads of glue into each of the bag. We began to sniff again. This time I totally blacked out. It was like I'd entered a large black void, mostly the same as the previous occasion though this time I had the craziest dreams. After what seemed like an age I remember slowly coming to. We were no longer at the swimming pool and instead on the main fairway of the golf course. My head felt like a merry-go-round. It was then I realised that John was swinging me around by my arm. I began to feel sick, regaining my senses quickly. John had a mad, distant look in his eyes. I tumbled over on the grass, tearing the knee of my jeans, the grass stain and bloody graze visible. Lying back and looking into the dusky sky. A sharp tug on my arm brought me back to my feet again. John swung around in circles; he was totally out of it and must have sniffed the remainder of the tin. I landed this time rolling down one of the banks of the course. I'd now got the fear. The dusk cast shadows on the course. Managing to get back on my feet I thought I'd better run. As I started running, John's arm caught me around the neck from behind. I was dragged to the floor. He pinned my arms down to the floor with my knees. Shit, I was in a tight spot, this youth was a nutter! Cloudy, vicious eyes regarded me with undiluted hate. 'I'm gonna strangle you, you cunt!', he bellowed. Sticky, glue covered hands were tight around my neck, the top of his gluebag visible from the top of his Donkey jacket. Try as I might I couldn't shift him. He was muttering, 'die you cunt', over and over. I thought this was the end of me, game over. He stopped, then grabbed my arm and threw me again, leaving me in a spluttering heap. He was soon back on top of me, as I tried to struggle my arms away from being pinned. The glue had totally worn off now, heart pounding. I punched him in the side and then had my hand pushing his hand back, this made him even more determined to continue his warped task. The brute strength pinned my arms down again. I was helpless. The hands were back around my throat, even though I'd been sniffing the miasma of glue and cigarettes were wafting onto me as he drew his face forward. This is it; I'm going to die, with thought of my previous life flashing through my mind. I was in the shit this time. Then John stopped, stood up and walked away. It was bizarre, yet I realised he must have come to and worked out what he was doing. I was angry, upset and still scared.

John made his way up the fairway to the exit gate, we'd been through earlier. I tagged along feeling the bruises appear around my neck and pulled muscles, adrenaline pulsing rapidly through my body. John was quiet, though I wanted answers. Catching up with him, I asked what the fuck was he up to. I was met with silence. He continued to walk saying nothing. Reaching the gate he stopped. I asked again, what all that violence was about. He still had a vacant look about him and muttered something about not knowing what I was on about. Fucking hell, he either had a very short memory or was in total denial of his actions. We gave each other a leg up over the fence and walked back towards my house pretty much in silence. My fuzzy head was clearing and I was beginning a plan of how I could get in the house and straight up to my room. It was way past ten O'clock now though my mother rarely complained about me being late in those days. Me and John parted company at the corner of Fellows Road, he only lived a few streets down. I mumbled something about seeing him again but made the mental note to avoid the mental cunt again at all costs. The realisation was hitting me clearly that I could have been killed. This sniffing thing could be fucking dangerous. Indeed that was an understatement.

Managing to get in the house undetected and mumbling something to my mother about getting an early night I got to my room. My reflection in the bathroom mirror betrayed the nasty bruises visible on my neck. I'd have to borrow some of my mother's foundation make up to cover them up. Looking at my torn knees in my jeans I felt lucky. I washed my grazed knee and went to bed. Sleep came fast that night, though the memory of this shitty night would last a lifetime. Monday at school, I avoided John, my mind firmly made up to avoid the mental bastard at all costs. That, in earnest was where our friendship stopped. Over the next few years we seldom saw each other and when we did the events of that night were never mentioned. My first sniffing session had been marked by the oblivion of total memory loss. I often puzzled that John's behaviour that night was down to his troubled background. That the past demons had come out to play in some glued up nightmare. I guess I'll never know.

The next few years were marked as most teenagers are, with fleeting trips across various friendship groups. My other love outside of punk rock during the early eighties was BMX freestyle bikes. This was the activity that kept me away from the sniffing, though as I matured, began to hang out with punks again. Glue inevitably revisited my life. Mostly my desire to sniff again was rekindled by schoolyard gossip of the older punks sniffing. The gluebags around the various nooks and crannies of Beeston multiplied and so did the tales. New peer groups were developing and I got into collecting punk records and also hanging about with a group of punks the same age. Steve, was one who was a decent sort of youth, we occasionally sniffed and had a laugh, mostly down the darker corners of the school field. The one tale of horror was one of the older punks who totally lost it whilst sniffing one night. The rumour was he totally damaged his brain and ended up in hospital. A lot of this was Chinese whispers of course though it turned out mixed with an equal measure of truth. With lots of the new peer groups forming at school, some were sniffing more regularly than others with some regularly skipping school to go down the Trent and spend the afternoon sniffing. One youth was expelled from the school as a result of being caught. He ended up at a school across the town.

The next group I fell into were ace. Mostly they were my own age and all into Discharge, Crass, UK82 but mostly anarcho punk. This would be my new peer group and I'd spend the next couple of years of my life hanging around with them. Central to the groups were the King brothers. Both shared a love of Stiff Little Fingers and we spent many a time walking home through the gluebag golf course, singing 'Wasted Life' and 'At the Edge' at the tops of our voices. What united us during late 1982 was a collective love of glue sniffing. The King Brothers both had paper rounds. More than that they were both excellent shoplifters. After their paper rounds they would both go into Wilkinson's hardware supermarket and lift a few tins of Evo Stick and packs of freezer-bags into their paper bags. By the time we split off after the walk home we agreed to meet at the Oak tree at the Golf Course entrance on Wollaton road at six. Sometimes we had to phone each other to check if the brothers had been successful in their Wilkos trip. The codename for glue in those days of parents listening into the landline was 'milk'. This 'code' saved our necks a couple of times as parents were sure we were up to no good.

Meeting at the Oak at six we were clearly had strength in numbers. There was anything from five to around twelve of us. We'd walk down Wollaton road, cross the A52 and head up through the sprawling Lowes estate to the scrubland at the back known as Snakey woods. Once there the sniffing began with the most popular spot being a tennis court on the school at the top. Things were much more relaxed and more punk than my past experiences of sniffing. My tolerance to sniffing had also improved. We could get really messed up yet remain in control. That wasn't to say that we didn't black out occasionally but I felt much safer doing it with these people. The years have blunted my memory somewhat though the residing memory for me at this point was the emergence of tunes filing my head as I sniffed. My favourite tune at this point was the Poison Girls 'Persons Unknown' track off the *Bloody Revolutions* split record with Crass. This tune repeated in my head throughout a number of sniffing sessions during the winter during early 1983. Equally and more bizarrely, I also had a music loop of Duran Duran's 'This is Planet Earth' stuck in my head whilst sniffing, enough to put me off the practice forever. I hated that fucking band. That said the general experience of sniffing glue at this time was my first experience of what could be achieved between a group of friends who were into punk. We all had our individual parental troubles and faced a bleak future in terms of jobs. Glue sniffing and punk was a great escape route for us as a group, a bonding ritual if you'll excuse the pun. In spite of other groups sniffing glue at school, our growing anarchist and vegetarian political stance brought the ire of the deputy headmaster and the local jocks. We managed to find strength in our status as outsiders. Gradually the sniffing tailed off for some of us, including myself as we approached leaving school. We were growing up fast and also getting heavily into animal rights politics. As glue was not vegetarian on account of its rather nasty animal bone ingredients, the practice fizzled out. After school most of us ended up either on government training schemes or on the dole. The last sniffing session I remember was just off Chilwell high road making our way down to Dovecote lane wreck. That night I remember the head sniffing soundtrack was from the Icons of Filth with the track 'Show us You Care'. That was a great memory, tainted only by the 'that's bloody disgusting' jibe from a passerby as I boldly sniffed in public walking down to Dovecote lane. My residing memories of this session were of one of the King brothers tripping into an altered state of consciousness on a glue high. This was the ultimate sought after glue sniffing experience. Schoolyard tales of hands coming out of gluebags; the glue man who came to visit the sniffers, holding conversations with them and the tale of three floating nuns one individual recounted. My own experience of this was sniffing at the Oak with a couple of mates one night when I evaporated into blue steam. I felt I'd left my body and vividly remember the feeling of looking back at myself in my donkey jacket and black Mohican haircut sniffing before materialising back in my body. That was an odd experience indeed.

Back on Dovecote lane wreck, the sniffing tailed off. A few had gone home on account of training schemes to attend the following day. I was left with the King brothers and a relative newcomer to the group: an ex Bramcote skinhead called Gramph, who'd seen the light of the anarcho punk ideal. He was also a frequent sniffer and had chased the King brothers once when they were sniffing up at Snakey woods. All was good now, or supposedly so. I was sat smoking on the swings, about to head off home. The others were in one of the wooden shacks built on the park for children to climb though. Grampher suddenly lost it lashing out unprovoked at the King brothers, the sound of punches resonating across the park. Various insults and threats were traded, though the fight soon calmed down. We parted and I took Grampher back up to my house to calm him down. Just like John he was oddly quiet and not recognising what had just occurred. The glare of the strip lights in the kitchen shone on the true state Grampher was in. He sat there not drinking the tea and moving his fingers in a circular motion, unresponsive to any of my questions. This seemed to go on forever, though I was mildly relieved when my mother entered the kitchen and he showed some signs of life. My previous experience with John nearly killing me left me nervous. The mental note had been made. Sniffing was a dangerous business. I was out of that hobby for good. Grampher eventually left and the incident never mentioned again. My time with this group of friends was beginning to move in different directions.

The year or so that followed our last sniff led me in a different path. I wanted to be a musician and took to hanging out in Rock City; this was where the occasional use of LSD in the mid eighties upstaged the gluebag days. One day we decided to return to Snakey to try sniffing again. After the mind-blowing blast of acid, most of us left and went our own ways. The teenage buzz was dead for us. Onto pastures new.

State Hate – Photo by Nigel Crouch

Everyone Was an Anarchist *Alistair Livingstone*

Metropolitan Warf, Wapping- home to the Autonomy Centre
1981-2

On 3 January 1979, in the middle of the so-called 'Winter of Discontent' I arrived at the London Rubber Company's east London factory to start a new job as a trainee draughtsman. I had started working for the company in one their factories in Gloucestershire in 1977. The year before, while I was briefly a student, I had joined an anarchist group at Stirling University and started buying Black Flag. I had also signed up to Stuart Christie's Ceinfeugos Press paying £2 a month to receive copies of the books they published.

A few months after arriving in London I was invited to a Black Flag/ Ceinfeugos readers meeting above a pub on the Kings Road. This turned out to be a support group meeting for the defendants in the Persons Unknown Anarchist Conspiracy Trial which was to begin in September, so as well as Stuart Christie and Albert Meltzer I met Iris Mills and Ronan Bennet and I think Dave Morris of later McLibel Trial was also there.

Iris and Ronan were acquitted and after the acquittal, Ronan had the idea of setting up an anarchist social centre in London. To raise funds for this social centre, the notionally anarchist punk groups Crass and the Poison Girls were approached to make a benefit record for the centre, which was released in 1980. As a result of this connection, at one of the planning meetings in early December 1979 I met a group of punks.

The meeting was held in the Conway Hall in Red Lion Square and after the meeting we all went to the nearest pub where I got into conversation with them and found that they produced a punk fanzine called 'Kill Your Pet Puppy'. I then started visiting the Puppy Collective at weekends and although I was only a part-time punk, became a regular contributor to the fanzine.

1978 -79 also saw a skinhead revival and the skinheads began attacking punk squats and disrupting punk gigs, including Crass ones. Rock Against Racism was very big in 1978 and overlapped with the Anti-Nazi League which was a Socialist Worker Party organisation. The National Front tried to counter this by setting up Rock Against Communism gigs which were popular with skinheads. In an attempt to distance themselves from what they saw as the politicisation of punk, Crass decided that they would become anarchists. This new stance was reflected in the lyrics of 'White Punks on Hope' written in early 1979.

Pogo on a Nazi, spit upon a Jew

Vicious mindless violence that offers nothing new

Left wing violence, right wing violence all seems much the same

Bully boys out fighting, it's just the same old game

Boring fucking politics that'll get us all shot

Left wing, right wing, you can stuff the lot

Keep your petty prejudice, i don't see the point

Anarchy and freedom is what i want

This did not solve the problem of violence at their gigs. This led Leigh Kendall, an Australian anarchist and punk to write a short article in Kill Your Pet Puppy number one, titled 'Peaceful Pro-Crasstination- a critical look at Crass peaceful anarchy stance and commitment to peaceful anarchism in relation to violence at their gigs'. Crass then invited Leigh and Tony Drayton to discuss the problem- which they did. It turned out that Crass had very little knowledge of anarchism. Penny Rimbaud of Crass was later to say

> In all honesty I wasn't aware of anarchism until about year one into Crass ...We had got a peace banner to tell people we weren't interested in kicking shit, and we had put up the circled A banner as something to get the left and right off our backs. It was then that we started getting people asking what we meant by that. I realised that outside of my own libertarian stance , I didn't know what the fuck it was about. It was then I started looking at what it actually meant in terms of its history. I hadn't had much interest in it and I can't say I have now to be honest.

In 1984, Andy Palmer of Crass told Radio Free France

> There were both left wing and right wing influences who were trying to co-opt what we were trying saying, which is largely why we adopted the anarchy symbol. Then we came up against the established anarchists, and their establishment idea of what anarchy meant, and as far as we could see, putting anarchy and peace together was a complete contradiction to the

idea of what they had of what anarchy was, which was chaos and no government, general violent revolution, which was the opposite of what we were trying to say. So we put the peace banner together with anarchy banner.

Crass' symbolic appropriation of 'anarchy' was already present at the very beginning of punk as Jon Savage explained several years later.

> There was a lot of talk about anarchy in the summer of 1976. John Lydon was working on a set of lyrics to one of Glen's tunes which became 'Anarchy in the UK'. Vivienne set about making a parallel item of clothing. The resulting 'Anarchy' shirt was a masterpiece. Taking a second-hand sixties shirt, Westwood would dye it in stripes, black, red, or brown., before stencilling on a slogan such as 'Only Anarchist Are Pretty' . The next stage was to stitch on more slogans, hand painted on rectangles of silk or muslin.. These made explicit references to Anarchist heroes and to the events of 1968 : 'Prenez vos desirs pour la realite', 'A bas le Coca Cola'.
>
> The final touches were the most controversial. Small rectangular portraits of Karl Marx (from Chinatown) were placed on the side of the chest, and on the other, above the pocket or on the collar, was placed an (often inverted) swastika from the Second World War. To ensure that the message was received, the whole shirt was finished off with an armband which simply read 'Chaos'. The intention was the group should not be politically explicit, but instead should be an explosion of contradictory, highly charged signs.

The Sex Pistols single 'Anarchy in the UK' was released in November 1976. The Crass and Poison Girls benefit single for what was to become the Wapping Autonomy Centre was released in May 1980 and raised £10 000 . The money was used to convert a space in a Victorian warehouse beside the Thames at Wapping into a social centre. After discussion the more neutral 'Autonomy Centre' was chosen over 'Anarchist Centre' as its name. It opened in early 1981 but was a rented space without an entertainment licence or a drinks licence. The rent was £680 a quarter and by November 1981 the lack of committed support from the traditional anarchist community had created a financial crisis.

To bring in some cash, it was agreed to put on punk gigs on Sunday nights at the Autonomy Centre. Over the next three month these brought in £700 but as Albert Meltzer sadly observed

> With the punks' money came the punks, and in the first week they had ripped up every single piece of furniture carefully bought, planned and fitted, down to the lavatory fittings that had been installed by Ronan Bennett from scratch, and defaced our own and everyone else's wall for blocks around. In the excitement of the first gigs where they could do as they liked, they did as they liked and wrecked the place. Loss of club, loss of money, loss of effort. End of story.

The problem was that the majority of the punks who came to the Sunday night gigs were teenagers, some as young as 13. Free for the night from home and school, they ran riot. For the slightly older punks and severa of the groups Autonomy Cemtre gigs were a continuation of gigs that had been put on in a squatted, derelict church on the Pentonville Road through 1980 and 81.These stopped after one of the homeless alcoholics who also used the church accidentally set fire to it.

While the end of the Wapping Autonomy Centre in February 1982 marked the end of one connection between anarchists and punks, a different connection soon emerged. The new connection was with a group of Spanish anarchists who had squatted an abandoned school on the Harrow Road called the Centro Iberico. The Spanish anarchists lived in the classrooms upstairs and allowed us to convert a former assembly room downstairs into a performance space. A stage was built using old cookers from the kitchens covered with carpet retrieved from skips. Although the Centro was evicted at the end of 1982, for a few month during the spring and summer it was used once a week for anarchist punk gigs. After that a series of 'Anarchy Centres' were squatted in north London over the next few years, one of which evolved into Molly's Café on Upper Street in Islington.

A spin-off from these activities was the setting up of the Black Sheep Housing Co-op in Islington in 1982, which by 1983 had been given four derelict houses to convert by Islington Council. After the failure of a building co-op to convert the houses, we had to do the conversion work ourselves. This venture provided an alternative to squatting for co-op members over the next ten years, although many of the original Black Sheep went on to become 'new age travellers'. I moved into one of the Black Sheep houses in 1983 while I was still working for London Rubber. Mark Wilson of the Mob, a well known anarcho-punk group lived in the same house and in 1984 Mark asked me to take over the Mob's record company called All the Madmen which I ran for the next couple of years and which I am still involved with 30 years on.

Politically, the some of the most interesting actions that took place in 1983/4 were the Stop the City protests. My partner Pinki, who I lived with from 1985 until her death in 1996 was involved in the planning of these protests. Pinki was brought up in Gloucester, but as soon as she was 16 in 1978, she left for London to become a punk, living in a series of squats. In 1980 she returned home and became involved with Stroud CND. In late 1981, Stroud CND visited the newly established peace camp at Greenham Common. The others went home but Pinki stayed at Greenham on and off for the next 3 years. In 1982 she took part in a protest against the Fallklands Victory Parade in London, which was organised by London Greenpeace.

In early 1983 Pinki was involved in the planning of the first Stop the City protest also organised by London Greenpeace where she was arrested and swiftly released since she was nine months pregnant. Her son Sky was born four days later. The full story of the Stop the City actions has yet to be written, but last year Rich Cross wrote about them for Freedom in September 2013.

> Called on 29 September 1983, to coincide with the quarterly calculation of the City's profits, protestors were encouraged to take part in a 'carnival against war' and deliver 'a day of reckoning' for the warmongers and racketeers of the Square Mile. Around 1500 anarchists, libertarians, punks and radical peace activists descended on the City to occupy buildings, block roads, stage actions and swarm through the streets.

> Cumulatively these efforts were designed to snarl up the operation of the capital's financial hub. In an analogue era, long before the City's 'Big Bang', when files and paperwork still had to be physically couriered between companies, the impact of mobs of unruly demonstrators filling

the City's narrow streets could be dramatic. Estimates differed, but the occupation of corporate space interrupted scores of monetary transactions, and drove down the day's profits. The cost to those demonstrating was significant too: more than 200 arrests at the first STC; nearly 400 at the March 1984 event; and close to 500 in September 1984.

Support for STC came from two principal directions: from elements within the radical wing of the nuclear disarmament movement (which had been looking for ways to generalise and extend action beyond military bases) and from within the ranks of anarcho-punk (a sub-culture eager to test out its collective political muscle). But the audacity of STC struck a chord with activists and militants from many other movements and campaigns.

Pinki was arrested again at the second Stop the City and held over night. A creche had been arranged and fortunately Dave Morris of London Greenpeace took Sky home with him after the creche closed. Pinki was arrested again on the third Stop the City, but this time we were in a relationship so she arranged that I would look after Sky for the day. Over the next 12 years, apart from 1990 when I almost stood for election as an anti-Poll tax Green Party councillor in Hackney, Pinki was the activist of the family while I kept the home fires burning. Pinki's last and 26th arrest was in June 1994 at a road protest in Bath.

Recently, while working on a talk for the Dunfries and Galloway branch of the Scottish Radical Independence Campaign I jotted down my memories of the Poll Tax in Hackney.

On 8 March the council met to set the poll tax rate for Hackney in a boarded up town hall surrounded by a wall of police confronting an increasingly agitated 1000 strong crowd. Three days earlier, Harringey had set their rate and there had been a minor riot. Now everyone was expecting a riot in Hackney. The whole scene was unreal. It didn't look or feel like everyday Hackney at all. I half expected helicopters to come in and rescue the councillors like what happened when Saigon finally fell to the Vietcong in 1974.

I had, rather naively, planned to give an election speech to the crowd so was wearing my wedding suit. There was a BBC London film crew there and I was chatting to them when they suddenly got busy, anticipating trouble. So I moved on to the steps in front of the town hall to get my speech in before the trouble started. I managed to say 'If you want to get rid of the Poll Tax, don't get mad get even and vote Green' before the police suddenly moved forward from behind me to push the crowd away from the town hall. The only response I had from my election speech was a young punk woman in the crowd shouting back at me 'It is too late for that now'.

I then went home then but my wife stayed on to report later that a riot had broken out. McDonalds burger bar was smashed up and Paddy Ashdown, who had been giving a speech in the Assembly Rooms behind the town hall, had his car attacked by the crowd and 38 people were arrested. One of our punk friends told us later that he had got close enough to Paddy Ashdown to give him a punch...

My enduring memory is of the few moments that I was stood between the police and the protestors, trying to give my political speech. The sheer intensity of the anger of the crowd was like a physical force, their rage, built up over 11 years of Thatcher governments waging class war was like a blazing furnace. It was not what I had expected at all. Like the young punk woman said, it was too late for my 'vote Green' pitch. Way too late. The only coherent thought I can recall from the experience was 'Fucking hell, there is going to be a revolution'.

But as I noted in my Radical Independence Campaign talk, reflecting on the dramatic events of 1990, it is possible to see in the very different reactions to the Poll Tax north and south of the Border the first signs that Scotland and the rest of the UK were beginning to move apart politically. In Scotland the economic hammer blows of Thatcherism reforged a powerful sense of Scotland as a civil society. Across most of England, the same hammer blows fractured the post-war consensus and fragmented civil society. In Scotland, the Poll Tax gave rise to a popular movement of collective resistance which also focused Scottish civil society on the need for constitutional change. This led to the creation of a devolved Scottish Parliament in 1999. In England the Poll Tax led to riots.

I then went on, wearing my historian's hat, to discuss the Scottish Enlightenment's concept of acivil society existing between individuals and families and the state. If there had still been a Scottish state with Edinburgh as its political centre, this idea might not have arisen. Scottish intellectuals would, as members of a privileged elite, have been part of this Scottish state. But with the new Union state of Great Britain centred on London, the dispossessed Scottish professors, lawyers and ministers had to re-invent themselves as members of their own stateless civil society.

In Europe, the idea of civil society was taken up by Georg Hegel. Hegel, however, developed his political 'Philosophy of Right' after the French Revolution and the Napoleonic wars. In Hegel's version, civil society emerged out the disintegration of the family as the focus of ethical life and in turn a rational state will emerge out of civil society as the 'actuality of the ethical idea'.

What Hegel hoped was that Prussia would be able to modernise and become a rational state without having to undergo a bloody revolution. But by the time he wrote an essay on the English (that is British) Reform Bill just before his death in 1831, Hegel was less optimistic. He feared that the forces unleashed by industrial capitalism would lead to revolution rather than reform in Britain.

Hegel's fear reminds me of a question Tony Drayton asked one of the veteran Spanish anarchists at the Centro Iberico in 1982. Tony asked him 'How did you manage to have an anarchist revolution in 1936?'. The reply was 'Everyone was an anarchist'. Hegel also once said that what is rational becomes real and what is real becomes rational. It is forty years since I became a 'self-confessed anarchist'. Over those years I have had plenty of time to change my mind. But I still believe that of all the varieties of political theories and practices, anarchism is the most rational and hence most real and so I look forward to the day when everyone is an anarchist.

Originally published MONDAY, MARCH 10, 2014

HTTP://GREENGALLOWAY.BLOGSPOT.CO.UK/2014/03/EVERYONE-WAS-ANARCHIST.HTML

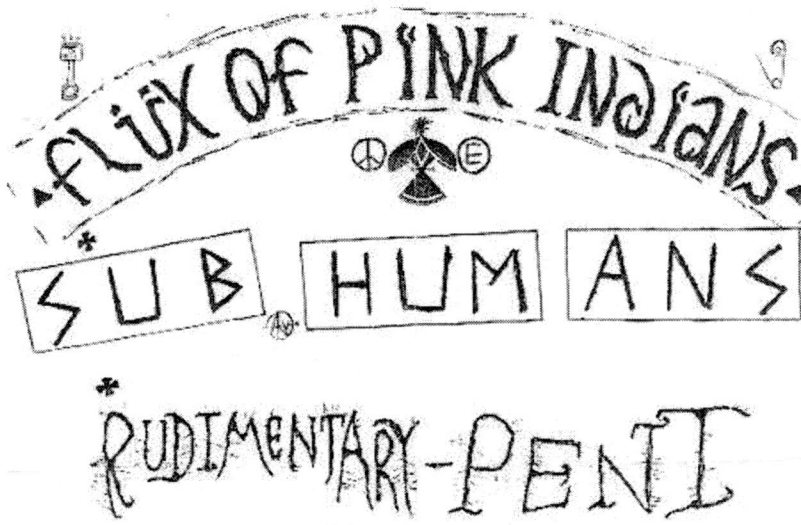

Gig Flyer by Persons Unknown

Golden Brown Market *Amanda Bigler*

"Heya! Get your cheese and dollies here. Get your darks, white horse, and gear. No lemonade, just China white and smack. No junk, just mother pearl and whack. Get your fix. Get your high. Get your trip. Come buy, come buy."

Lizzie and Laura strode, arms linked, across the darkened town square. Their heels clipped against the worn market street in a percussion of clip-clop, clip-clops. Their fingers laced together against the autumn wind. The call of the dealer, though cracked and raspy with cold, was coated in an air of euphoria. Lizzie drew her thick woolen scarf up past her nose and stared down at the jigsaw pieces of stone below her. Laura glanced toward the thin, swaying man, looking at his figure through lacquered lashes. Her pace slowed and her eyes fixed on the bundles at the hustler's feet. Clip-clop, swish-clasp, crack-rasp.

"Look, Lizzie. Look, Lizzie!"

"Don't look, Laura," Lizzie whispered harshly. "No, no, no."

"I'm not, I'm not," Laura replied.

Lizzie pushed at Laura's arm. Lizzie could feel her pulse beating against Laura's warm hand, and she knew her heart would not calm until the shouts of the street man were far behind them. Laura blushed, adrenaline coursing into her apple cheeks. Her curiosity had been stoked by the pusher's tone, and she wondered what forbidden goods could cause such a brilliant semblance of bliss. Lizzie's face went pale at her sister's expression, the blood sinking to her feet.

"What was that back there, Laura?" Lizzie asked, locking the door of their flat.

"Nothing," Laura said, unstrapping her shoes and spreading her toes out against the ragged, worn carpet in the living room. "Really, it was nothing. It's just, it was a hard day at work today, you know, and his voice... his voice was just so, peaceful."

"Of course it was peaceful, Laur. He was obviously high on God knows what."

Lizzie threw her keychain onto the linoleum pasted countertop. Clink-shhhh-thump. It slid off the surface and fell to the floor. She reached down to retrieve it.

"I know, I know. But don't you ever wonder... ever wonder what it'd feel like? I've heard it's like heaven on earth; that it's like all troubles in the world just disappear."

The keys dropped once more in Lizzie's shaking grasp. Her throat constricted at Laura's words. She abandoned the chain and marched over to her sister, grabbing her shoulders tightly.

"I never, ever, have wondered what sticking a needle full of drugs into me would feel like. You're really starting to scare me with this. Just let it go, please?"

At the sight of Lizzie's pleading, misty eyes, Laura lay down on the couch and turned on the ancient television set in the corner. Without looking at her sister, she forced the excitement from her voice.

"Yeah, Liz, sure. I didn't really mean it. It's just, you know, it crosses my mind sometimes."

"Stay away from that stuff, Laura. Please?"

"Okay, sure."

Lizzie picked up the keys, re-locked the door with a shhh-swish-click, and retired to her bedroom. Laura spent the night on the couch, watching the television program without seeing. No matter how much she tried, she could not expel the want her body possessed. She could not forget the sound of the man's voice. When the first dreary rays of muted sunlight peeked through the blinds, Laura's resolve was cemented. The temptation of ecstasy was too great for her to ignore.

The next evening after a night of rowdy pub patrons, a thinly veiled suggestive pass from the manager, and an electric bill notice discovered in her pocket, Laura remained determined to initiate her plan. Lizzie had watched Laura throughout the shift, her concerned looks dodged and unanswered by her sister.

"You sure everything's alright, Laur?" Lizzie had asked, ten minutes before the clock set them free.

"Table two needs washing," was Laura's reply, rubbing a booth down rigorously.

The two ventured into the street, arms locked as always and fingers entwined against the bitter air. Lizzie waited with bated breath for the hustler's nightly cries. Laura strained her ears, her impatience swelling up within her in painful anticipation.

"Heya! Where your chip is, where your cotics are. Get your golden brown, gamot, and black tar. No fluff, just blue velvet and Teddies. No bad bundles, just big H and Betties. Get your fix. Get your high. Get your trip. Come buy, come buy!"

"Go home, Lizzie. I'll meet you there."

"Laura, no! I can't let you. Remember Jeanie? Remember what happened to her after messing with that stuff? She died, Laura. I planted daisies on her grave. They won't even grow. She died."

But Laura's eyes were dewy in the dim lamplight of the street. She let go of Lizzie's hand, running up to the pusher and leaving her sister forgotten in the street. Lizzie rested her back against an empty building wall, closing her eyes to the interaction in front of her. Rasp-swish-thud. The anger rushed into her cheeks, her temples screaming with betrayal. She shoved her empty fingers into her pockets, and ran the rest of the way back, forcing herself to keep her eyes to her feet.

"Heya girl, you want to try? I'll give you a taste."

"I don't have any money. I gave it to my sister for the bills," Laura said, her voice shaking with desperate hope into the man's black eyes.

"First do up's on the house, along with the kit."

The man's cadence flowed through her, and she set down on the cold ground as the man bid. He dug through his bag, abstracting a tourniquet, needle, and vial. At his instruction, Laura rolled up her sleeve. The rubber constricted against her bicep, making her arm tingle and her veins bulge. With a tink-tink-shhhip, he slid the point into her. The bite of the metal was sated by the wonderfully warm sensation pouring through. It was sweeter than honey squeezed from a rock, stronger than perfectly fermented wine. Clearer than water, the juice flowed through her. Not knowing whether it was night or day, she left the man and turned home alone.

"Laura!" Lizzie shrieked as she opened the door to her sister's limp stance.

"Lizzie, let me sit on the couch. I've tasted the most amazing thing. It cost me nothing, and now I'm floating. I took all he would give me, and I'm going back tomorrow for more. You'll love it, Lizzie, the dishes of gold, too heavy for me to hold. You'll love it, Lizzie, odorous mead and lilies at the brink…"

Laura kissed Lizzie, a sweetly slow and childlike thing. She slumped onto the couch, reaching her hand out for her sister. Lizzie took it in hers, tears spilling down her cheeks at the sight of the bright red dots lining Laura's arm. The lullaby of their childhood rang through their minds and rocked them to sleep. Golden head by golden head, they lay there together that night, crushed in an embrace of paradise and hell.

The next morning broke over the sisters, the cool sun whipping against the window pane. Lizzy's face was puffed from crying. Laura's forehead burned with ache.

"Oh God, you're knocking at Death's door."

"Lizzy, please," Laura said with a quiver, blearily looking up at her sister, "please go to the market, please."

"I can't Laura, I can't go there. I don't want it. I don't need it. I don't want you to have it."

"I need it. I have to have it, Lizzie. Please, go for me. Please."

At the look at her sister's pale face, at the remembrance of poor Jeanie and her demise through her withdrawal, she nodded shortly and headed outside. Laura smiled, knowing soon she would be back in heaven. Knowing her sister was the angel to bring her there. Clip-clack-bang, and the door closed.

"Heya! Get your brother, dirt, and chick. Get your schmeck, aries, and shit. No flea powder, just China cat and bindle. No ragweed, just red rum and hazel. Get your fix. Get your high. Get your trip. Come buy, come buy."

"I need to get some, well, something for my sister."

His look was evil.

"She's the one that cut out before. You can pay me with company."

"I'm not going to do this. I'm getting it for her. I don't want to do it."

He wrestled her to her hands and knees, trying to tie the tourniquet around her still-clothed arm. He trod and hustled her, elbowed and jostled her. He clawed with his nails. He tore her gown, and twitched her hairs out by the root. She slapped at his face, digging with her fingernails. He howled in frustration. Spotting a filled syringe, Lizzy grabbed for the gleaming glass vial. Aiming at the man's unclothed arm, she jabbed the needle into his flesh. As animated as he had been, he immediately collapsed to the pavement with a sickening crack. Lizzie took a package from the unconscious man's bag and ran back home.

"Laura? Laura, wake up. I have something for you. Please, please wake up."

At her sister's lifeless body, she flinched. Taking the vial from the bag, she injected the needle with the golden weight of the liquid. Closing her eyes, she jabbed her sister with the syringe. Laura did not move. Shaking with anguish, fear, and pain, she kissed and kissed Laura with a hungry mouth. She pressed on her bosom and caressed her dull fingertips. Lizzie rested her hands when Laura's ribcage stilled. Pleasure passed and anguish passed, and Laura's dull eyes stared past Lizzie into the golden brown waves.

Inspired By:

(1830-1894), Christina Georgina Rossetti. "Goblin Market" Books & Literature Classics. http://classiclit.about.com/library/bl-etexts/crossetti/bl-crossetti-goblin.htm (accessed March 2, 2013).

Kelvin "Cal" Morris - Discharge – by Jacky Smith

"The Outcasts: Punk in Northern Ireland during the troubles." *Francis Stewart*

http://www.youtube.com/watch?v=DruhJkZU4EI (Good Vibrations trailer)

Good Vibrations[5] is an independent movie that seeks to illustrate through the use of familiar tropes the importance of music as a transformative experience. The above trailer demonstrates the centrality of punk music as a means of change through relationships, do-it-yourself, and resistance. The movie is based on the life of Terri Hooley, specifically his role in the nascent punk scene in Belfast as something of an unlikely hero and ringmaster. In focusing on Hooley the movie serves up a number of points key to this chapter: the power of music to sidestep divisions and boundaries;[6] the troubles in Northern Ireland as a background in everyday life;[7] the ability within punk to cherry pick aspects and times and conveniently ignore or marginalise other equally important but less 'sellable' dimensions.[8]

This chapter will be structured to deal with each of these three areas as a means of demonstrating that Northern Ireland had[9] one of the most vital and vibrant punk scenes in the UK at the time of the troubles. Vital in that, it was often the only space for Catholics and Protestants to mix and interact.[10] Vibrant in that it was largely isolated from the drama and media wrangling of the mainland punk scenes and so had to form and inform itself.[11] The chapter is based on the auto-ethnography of the author and on a sociological and religious studies research project on punk during and after the troubles.[12]

Troubles as a backdrop

The first punk band I saw live was Stiff Little Fingers (SLF) in Belfast in 1993. On the way to the venue I passed graffiti that read "Can you hack a pastie supper Bobby?",[13] "No surrender, remember

---

[5] 2013, directed by Lisa Barros D'Sa and Glenn Leyburn, distributed by The Works
[6] David Cooper, *The Musical Traditions of Northern Ireland and its Diaspora*, (Surrey: Ashgate, 2009); Desmond Bell, *Acts of Union: Youth Culture and Sectarianism in Northern Ireland*, (Hampshire: MacMillian, 1990) p8; Sean O'Neill & Guy Trelford, *It Makes You Want To Spit*, (Dublin: Reekus Music, 2003)
[7] Marc Mullholland, *The Longest War: Northern Ireland's Troubled History*, (Oxford: Oxford University Press, 2002); Martin Dillon, *The Shankill Butchers: A Case Study of Mass Murder*, (London: Arrow Books, 1990); Susan MacKay, *Northern Protestants: An Unsettled People*, (Belfast: Blackstaff Press, 2000)
[8] Martin McLoone, Punk Music in Northern Ireland: The Political Power of 'What Might Have Been', *Irish Studies Review*, Vol.12, No. 1, 2004 pp29 – 38; Andy Medhurst, *What Did I Get? Punk, Memory and Autobiography*, in Punk Rock: So What? Edited by Roger Sabin, (London: Routledge, 1999) pp219 -231; Daniel S. Traber, *L.A.'s "White Minority": Punk and the Contradictions of Self-Marginalization*, Cultural Critique, No. 48 (Spring 2001) pp30 - 64
[9] I would argue still has in some respects.
[10] O'Neill & Trelford, 2003, pV; McLoone, 2004, p35; Francis Stewart, *Alternative Ulster: Punk Rock as a Means of Overcoming Religious Divide in Northern Ireland*, in *Irish Religious Conflict in Comparative Perspective* edited by John Wolffe (Hants: Palgrave MacMillian, Forthcoming April 2014).
[11] http://news.bbc.co.uk/1/hi/northern_ireland/7797071.stm (last accessed 30.07.2011); Ian Glasper, *Burning Britain: The History of UK Punk 1980 – 1984*, (London: Cherry Red Records, 2004) p346
[12] Used within this chapter are excerpts from 13 preliminary interviews and extended conversations. All interviewees were aged between 35 and 50 to ensure they had grown up and been involved with punk during the troubles. They were all from Belfast, or had spent a considerable period of their adult life living there. They were a mix of male and female and were, with two exceptions, working class both as children and as adults.
[13] This is in reference to the death of the Republican hunger striker and MP Bobby Sands who died at the age of 24 in May 1981. He was on hunger strike as a protest against the removal by the British Government of the "political

1690"[14] and "Ulster says No".[15] These were not phrases that caused me to consciously stop and think, instead they acted as a referent to what Neil Jarman describes as "social memory".[16] An *"understanding of past events that are remembered by individuals, but within a framework structured by the larger group."*[17] Before I had left home I had checked news reports for bombs, bomb scares and so on as this would tell me where traffic disruption would be and whether buses and trains were running as timetabled. This was standard practise for any event you planned to attend, or even for simple everyday activities such as getting to and from school or work, doing the shopping and so on.

On a day to day basis the troubles were a backdrop, something that you had to bear in mind and be alert to, but also something that just was. That is not to, in any way, deny or denigrate the suffering that many individuals, families and communities endured. There was a sustained campaign by paramilitaries on both sides to disrupt life as much as possible. The scale of injury and loss of life during the troubles – over 3700 people died – is horrific, and the impact long reaching. However it also resulted in those outside of it focusing on the violence and those who cause it / have power to speak on it. The voice and experience of the ordinary person *"do not carry sufficient authority, and often go unheeded."*[18] Consequently, or arguably concurrently, ordinary people simply deal with the violence and fear that surrounds them by doing what they can to maintain a semblance of normality in their everyday life. This approach is comparable with how ordinary citizens live and think in areas of intense civil war, as for example Israel / Palestine[19] or Libya[20].

In relation to the concerns of this chapter – punk music in Northern Ireland during the troubles – there was a very direct impact. Often bands would avoid Northern Ireland (some even the Republic of Ireland) on their tours. This was especially true after the brutal massacre of The Miami Showband in Buskhill on the 31st July 1975. The popular cabaret band were returning to Dublin after a performance and were stopped by a bogus army checkpoint set up by the paramilitary group the Ulster Volunteer

---

prisoner" status assigned to arrested members of paramilitary groups and the removal of the privileges that designation brought. A pastie supper is a popular meal which consists of pork, onion and potato combined, battered, deep fried and served with chips. The term 'hack' is a colloquialism that means undertake or successfully complete a challenge. The sentence is also the title and chorus of a popular loyalist song / jingle written after the death of Sands.

[14] 1690 refers to the Battle of the Boyne and is specifically remembered by Loyalists and Protestants as the date of King William of Orange's victory and thus the symbolic victory of Protestantism over Catholicism.

[15] A refrain often used by prominent Protestants such as Rev Ian Paisley, particularly at rallies and to the media. It grew in significant popularity after the Anglo-Irish Agreement of 1985.

[16] Neil Jarman, *Material Conflicts*, (Oxford Berg: 1997) p4

[17] Jarman, 1997, p6

[18] Marie-Therese Fay, Mike Morrissey & Marie Smyth, *Northern Ireland's Troubles: The Human Costs*, (London: Pluto Press, 1999) p2

[19] Daniel Bar-Tal, *The Necessity of Observing Real Life Situations: Palestinian – Israeli violence as a laboratory for learning about social behaviour*, European Journal of Social Psychology, Volume 34, Issue 6, 2004, pp677 – 701; Julie Peteet, *Male Gender and Rituals of Resistance in the Palestinian Intifida: a cultural politics of violence*, American Ethnologist, Vol 21 No 1, (Feb 1994), p31 -49, pp35.

[20] Lindsey Hilsum, Sandstorm: Libya in the Time of Revolution, (London: Faber & Faber, 2012) pp1 -39

Force who attempted to put explosives onto their van. It exploded prematurely, killing two. The remaining paramilitaries opened fire on the band killing three and injuring two.[21]

Tragedies such as this created a fear of touring into the country and many bands would not receive insurance cover if they did come. However 20th October 1977 marked a seminal moment for some in Northern Ireland. The Clash was due to play the Ulster hall. A first of its kind event, a leading English punk band playing in Northern Ireland – Belfast no less – at least it was until the council cancelled it.[22] When the fans found out a near riot ensued and the army were brought in to disperse the angry crowd.[23] Although The Clash returned a number of times after that, an important lesson was indelibly etched into the psyche of young punks – the troubles meant they were on their own. They had to create their own scene in the midst of civil war. Brian Young, from the band Rudi, sums it up:

> *Years of what have been euphemistically referred to as 'the troubles' had taken their toll. Town centres shut down at night and people just didn't mix outside of their own communities. The N.I. music industry was stone dead and no one half decent was brave or foolhardy enough to play here. Yet, paradoxically, this provided the perfect breeding ground for punk. A whole new generation of restless, bored, alienated and frustrated teens had grown up here, going nowhere*

---

[21] http://www.themiamishowband.com/tag/the-miami-showband-massacre/ (last accessed 02.01.14); Stephen Travers & Neil Fetherstonhaugh, The Miami Showband Massacre: A Survivor's Search for the truth, (London: Hodder Headline Publishing, 2007)

[22] There are numerous rumours as to who was actually responsible for the cancelling of the gig – the council because of fear of noise or the army / police because of a fear of anti-social behaviour and a large gathering of belligerent people. No official documents exist to confirm either way, and it was likely a combination of both, however I have written council here as they had the power to officially revoke a playing licence.

[23] Johnny Green & Garry Barker, *A Riot of Our Own: Night & Day with The Clash,* (London: Orion Books, 1997) p23; http://www.theclashblog.com/the-clash-in-belfast-1977/ (last accessed 02.01.14)

fast, in what felt like the most fucked up and pitiful country on the planet – and punk was the perfect antidote! ... Ulster punk evolved into a totally unique and resilient hybrid that punched way above it's weight and went on to confound and exceed even our wildest expectations. By necessity, Ulster punk was DIY all the way.[24]

Brian's words bring us to the next section of this chapter, forming their own community within a deeply fractured and divided society necessitated finding something that could transcend those fissures and differences. For many of the young people into punk it was located in the music, in the ethics, in the attitude and the politics.

Sidestepping division and boundary

I suppose how I would describe it now is that, like, punk transcended religion so it did. You know like, like it was something else to focus on, something that we had in common. We were the outsiders so why make yourself even more on the outside by focusing on religion. Punk was far more important than that so it was. You get what I mean? Like by having this thing in common we could, I dunno, get past the religion thing, see the person behind it and they really weren't all that different from the rest of us so they weren't. Colin 02.12.09

In the above section I mentioned going to see SLF as my first live punk experience. As everyone did I arrived with the baggage of the situation I grew up in, although I barely registered the graffiti I had walked past or the murals I had seen, I knew what they meant and the message behind them. I went to a school that was segregated on gender, education ability and religious identity, these divisions were all I knew. However, that night it all changed, the audience was mixed and willingly so. To my ever-lasting shame I have no memory of the supporting band at all because I was so busy making sure I knew where the exits where for when the inevitable fight broke out between the Catholics and Protestants, as I assumed it would. It never did and when SLF hit the stage and I was wrapped up in the wall of sound I didn't care about divisions and boundaries, the person dancing next to me was just that – a person. The song 'Alternative Ulster'[25] took on so many new meanings that night.

For me, the music and the lyrics were transformative and a number of other interviewees made similar comment.

The music, it was, is, amazing, there is just something about it. I play drums and every time I hit those skins it's like I hit out another part of the shite I grew up with, you know what I mean? Kinda like it takes you to another place, shows that there is something else besides hatred and death and bombs and crap. (Dylan 15 July 2010)

The music, it grabs you and doesn't let go. It makes it ok to be angry, to want change. Listen, its exhausting going round that pit, dancing like that but you have to, you want to, the music compels you. And even though you're knackered at the end of it you aren't the same person, you have changed somehow. (Deb 2 November 2010)

---

[24] Brian Young quoted in O'Neil & Trelford, 2003, p262
[25] 'Alternative Ulster', Stiff Little Fingers, Inflammable Material, 1979, Rough Trade

You couldn't escape religion or politics and if you ignored them it could cost you your life, but for a few hours a night, playing that music, being with your mates, slamming in the pit, sitting in your room listening to tapes, the world came alive for a while. Like yeah, like I had for the first time ever something I could believe in, you know? (Julie 28 July 2011)

Although expressed in different terms, and related specifically to their own context, the interviewees above reveal the ability of music to be transformative in ways analogous with the three means noted by music researcher and philosopher Jeanette Bicknell. Those three being; physical reactions *"a clear marker of strong experience ... significant because they are clear indications that the music has overcome listeners and undermined their defences"*[26]; social feelings and connections; a feeling of or connection with the sublime or ineffable.[27]

This clip from the Good Vibrations movie demonstrates all three of these effects as Terri Hooley discovers Rudi playing their song "Big Time" and is captivated, transported and altered by the experience. For those unfamiliar with the movie or indeed the man, Hooley is the slightly older gentleman with the beard. http://www.youtube.com/watch?v=YTGrGde7G68 It is worth noting here that the effects of the music on the individual, and indeed the group, can be long lasting – Hooley did indeed release 'Big Time' for Rudi (although he famously forgot to include the actual record when he initially sent the sleeves to radio stations) – or short lived. After Rudi leave, Hooley is approached by another band The Outcasts who ask him to release them, his response is "I'm not that pissed." The music hasn't affected him quite that much![28]

The impact of music on individuals by enabling them to shift their perspective, engage with and express emotions is of course important, however we also need to examine the use of music to build community. In a society as fractured and suspicious as Northern Ireland community was intensely important and protected. Desmond Bell writes, *"Young people in NI develop a sense of ethnic awareness in an ongoing situation of political mobalization and sectarian confrontation. Historically conditioned cultural divisions are reproduced in and through the education system. Increasing levels of segregation combined with the isolating effect of mass unemployment have led to further ghettoization of young people within their confessional communities."*[29]

Bell continues to argue persuasively that the generation who formed the early punk scene in Northern Ireland were affected far more than their parent's generation. This is due to their birth coinciding with the onset of the troubles resulting in a lack of mobility in a physical sense as well as economic, thus hindering their recreational activities. However his quick dismissal of dissonant styles and subcultures such as punk (he also includes mods, rockers and skins) as being solely the product of

---

[26] Jeanette Bicknell, *Why Music Moves Us,* (Hampshire: Palgrave MacMillian, 2009) p48
[27] Bicknell, 2009, p48 – 60
[28] Although it should be noted that later Hooley did sign The Outcasts to his Good Vibrations label for three years 1978 – 1981. The Outcasts split in 1985 but played the Rebellion Festival in 2011 and sporadically in Belfast since. Ian Glasper features them in his book 'Burning Britain: The History of UK Punk 1980 -1984' p352 - 359
[29] Desmond Bell, *Acts of Union: youth sub-culture and ethnic identity amongst Protestants in Northern Ireland,* The British Journal of Sociology, Vol 38, No 2, June 1987 p158 – 183 pp158

commercial interest and media hard sell and thus a foreign import to be disregarded as 'un-Irish'[30] is to misunderstand and marginalise youth counter culture movements and their importance in areas such as Northern Ireland.

Ian Murdock, vocalist with The Defects explains the punk community at the time; *"All the punks got on really well. Both Protestants and Catholics, the only real religion was punk. There was never any rivalry between us and any of the other bands either; both The Outcasts and Rudi let us support them many times. We all hung about together, and musically we just wrote about what we saw and coming from Belfast we obviously saw different things than what you would see on the mainland."*[31]

Many interviewees commented on a sense of togetherness and / or developing their own community within.

You had to work together, there was precious few of us and we seemed to be a target for every sod. You got the police at you for anti-social, your teachers and parents at you for being yourself and spides and skins that wanted to kick your head in everytime they saw you just cause of how you looked. So yeah you didn't go looking for yet more differences in those around you, you stuck together and over time that became its own community. (Nathan 3 May 2010)[32]

Allegiances that's how I would describe it really. You grew up on one side or the other, you got no say in that and it decided who your friends could be, what schools you went to and what have you. But then you could go see these bands play, and they were usually just your mates unless you got the big ones like Rudi or The Outcasts or the huge ones like Fingers – I never rated the Undertones so I never bothered with them and suddenly none of that mattered. You liked people simply because they liked the same music as you, they dressed like you, got hassled about it same as you did and would stick up for you in a fight. Suddenly you got to pick a side, you got to say this is who I am and my allegiances lie with punk and with the punks, they are my community you know. It's hard to get that across like in terms of how monumental that was, cause just no-one done it before that I knew of. (Patrick 13 July 2010)

Right ok well I'm trying dead hard here to get it into the right words, I know this is gonna be read by those not into punk and not from here and I really want them to understand just how important and radical it was to create a community that wasn't based on division or them and us but on a love for a style of music. It didn't divide, it united. It gave us something new, you know? (Phil 27 July 2011)

---

[30] Ibed p159
[31] Ian Murdock quoted in Ian Glasper, *Burning Britain: The History of UK Punk 1980 – 1984*, (London: Cherry Red Records, 2004) p346
[32] A spide is the Northern Irish colloquial term for an individual who in England would be known as a Chav [council housed and violent] and in Scotland as a NED [non-educated delinquent]. These are typically derogatory terms reserved for those who behave in loutish ways and dress to indicate their own self-emphasis on low class and low education.

Both the importance of tradition and the close-knit community cannot be overstated. To be a punk was to stand out, to be noticed and therefore to become a target so strength in numbers is a means of protection, a form of security in an insecure environment. In addition to be a punk is to be different from the past. Punk, and its adherents, create and maintain significant behaviours and ideals; an anarchic do-it-yourself ethos, sneering dismissal of self-appointed authority and the desire to reject or refute tradition. For many mainland UK punks the latter of these was a rejection of rules and hierarchy of the music business, in Northern Ireland tradition has an entirely different meaning. Tradition is often a means of demarcating political, cultural and religious identity, allegiance and territory.

Consequently, in Northern Ireland the desire to reject or refute tradition transmuted into a rejection of the entrenched partisan politics of their parent's generation and a rejection of the violent sectarian politics of paramilitary groups. Segregation was irrelevant; it was anathema to punk's ethos of all can do it. Catholics, Protestants and atheists co-mingled, interacted, danced and played together. This was not limited to venues, performances were vacated in mixed groups, friendships were maintained socially in the city centre and protected when attacked. At first it was a political statement just to gather together so when they were stopped by police checks or rounded up during a gig, it was often with a perverse delight that they revealed they were mixture of Catholic and Protestant, with a plethora of addresses proving it.

> *It was a political statement just to go to the Harp and pogo to some decent music back then. Political cause we all just mixed together and that wasn't encouraged wasn't allowed.* (Tommy, 7 April 2011)

> *There was no sense of religion amongst ourselves. No-one ever asked where you lived or came from. We didn't care about addresses or religions.* (Colin 2 February 2009)

> *This one time, we got stopped by the army. Random checks me arse! They checked us all and then wanted names and addresses. Shoulda seen their faces as we reamed them all off – Falls Road, Sydenham, Short Strand and the GlenBurn estate. It was class! One of the soldiers told us we should form our own political group!* (Gordon 1 December 2009)

> *Ah yeah (laughs) the p-stops, their faces when we used to reveal the places we lived. We'd crossed the divides, we didn't care so it was such a geg that they did.* (Deb 2 November 2011)

It cannot be over-emphasised the role that punk music itself played in this. It was the reason why these young people were coming together, were breaking with tradition and forging new bonds of friendship and loyalty. Musicologist Tia DeNora argues that this is because of music's ability to be utilised *"as a means of organizing potentially disparate individuals such that their actions may appear to be intersubjective, mutually orientated, co-ordinated, entrained and aligned."*[33]

In effect, these punks were creating their own 'imagined community' that existed outside of, or parallel to, the divided and traumatised communities they lived in.[34] Imagined communities, according

---

[33] Tia DeNora, *Music in Everyday Life,* (Cambridge: Cambridge University Press, 2000) p109
[34] Benedict Anderson, *Imagined Communities,* (London: Verso, 1983)

to Benedict Anderson, are so called *"because the members of even the smallest nation will never know most of their fellow-members, meet them, or even hear of them, yet in the minds of each lives the image of their communion."*[35] In other words commonality is assumed rather than proven to such an extent that those assumptions become ingrained. Thus to claim a punk identity is to claim membership of that imagined community which leads other to presume that you agree with their understandings of ideas, actions and memories. I would argue that this results in a two-fold consequence; first, the strengthening of a small community in a dangerous environment, second the ability or reason why punk is so selective in how it is remembered. It is the latter that the final section will focus on before drawing some conclusions.

Cherry picking and rose tinted glasses

There is a tendency within punk itself, as well as by the broader media and those who study popular culture, to cherry pick the more successful or sellable elements and remember them to such an extent that all else is lost. In addition in a scene as small a Northern Ireland there can be a proclivity towards assuming that the imagined community was one of harmony due to size and external pressure. These are the two issues this final section will engage with.

Ian Glasper's series of books[36] are a remarkable reminder of why the documenting of the variety and scope of punk bands in various era and cities the length and breadth of the UK is of paramount importance. They remind us that it is human nature to divide, to categorise, to pigeon hole. We do this because it enables us to understand, to control and to try to ensure that we keep the best for ourselves. Punk scenes are no different, despite what we may like to tell ourselves, so a reminder of the variety is vital to help prevent complete co-option and ensure an honest and full history.

The tendency for Northern Irish punk to be focused on SLF, the Undertones and Good Vibrations results in important areas such as the Warzone collective not being acknowledged. The risk then is that groups such as this are not supported by the community and so not around for the next generation of punks. Key to developing a strong sense of community and cohesion in a country rife with division was the creation of centres in which young people could gather and talk, hang out and be safe. The precursor to the Warzone was the short lived A centre or Anarchy centre in Belfast city centre in 1981. It was run by the Belfast Anarchist Collective and was responsible for providing such a space during afternoons – particularly a Saturday afternoon.

> *The Centre brought bands such as Crass, Dirt and Poison Girls to the province, and also provided a venue for local bands such as Rudi, The Defects, Dogmatic Element, and Stalag 17. They also showed films such as 'One Flew Over The Cuckoo's Nest', 'Monty Python's Life of Brian' and 'Rude Boy'.*[37]

---

[35] Ibid p6
[36] Burning Britain (mentioned above); The Day The Country Died (2006); Trapped in a Scene (2009); Armed with Anger (2012)
[37] O'Neil & Trelford, 2003, p2

The constant army and police raids forced the centre to close after 6 months. During that time they provided a clear link between ideas of having things done for you by co-operations to whom you are then beholden to and do them yourself, the diy punk ethos. The Anarchy centre was an example of diy in action for many young punks. Sadly very few images from the time exist but below are a front cover from the fanzine they produced and a still from the movie they shot about the centre.

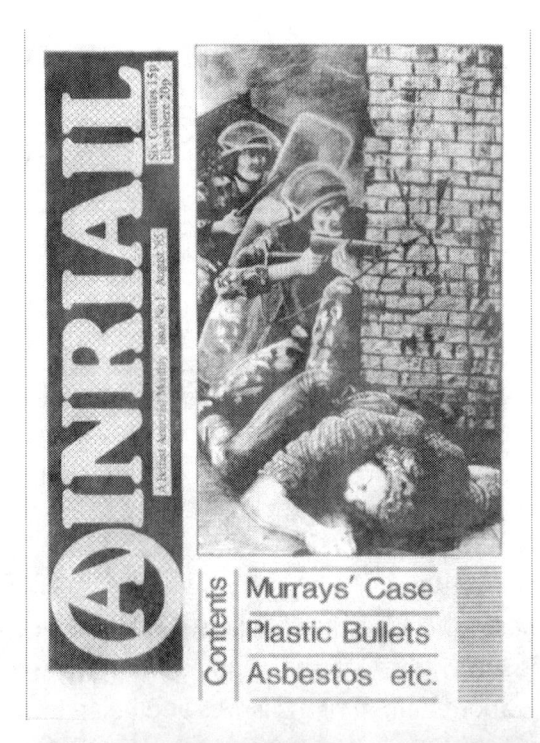

In a similar vein to the Anarchy centre there is Giro's, now known as The Centre, which acts in a similar manner although it is not structured around Anarchy per se, but is more broadly interested in catering for a wide range of punk tastes such as hardcore / emo / straight edge and metalcore. In addition to hosting bands and providing a place for vegan food, the Centre in 2011 also opened itself up to providing a practice space and screen printing facilities. Below is the flyer from this event.

The centre is overseen and run as a collective on a volunteer basis by Warzone, who are an anarchy based organisation. Warzone began in 1984 on the dual basis of DIY and that beliefs should impact into our actions. As such then the principle of live and let live is shown through their commitment to creating and serving vegan food, providing a voice and information about animal rights issues and being involved in hunt sabotaging. For them, this is a key part of their anarchic principles and an important part of being a community. This link will take readers to their website for further information and some copies of their fanzine which they continue to publish. http://warzonecollective.com/?page_id=2

However, as mentioned above, being a part of an imagined community not only promotes togetherness and protection, but also risks marginalising important voices and so not having a complete history. In addition, the presentation on community within this chapter could easily lead to the assumption that it was one solid community that stood alone against the varying forces – a living us versus them. Creating such an impression would be specious and again prevent the development of a complete history.

There were of course conflicts – between bands, between fans and participants, between musical ideas and between ideologies. For example, Stiff Little Fingers were criticised by the Undertones for glamorising the troubles, while Stiff Little Fingers countered with the accusation that the Undertones ignored the troubles.[38] It is worth noting that the Undertones "It's Going to Happen" is about the hunger strikes at the Maze prison and after the death of Bobby Sands, Damian wore a black armband to perform on Top of the Pops.[39] It is possible that it was actually sectarianism that drove the wedge

---

[38] O'Neil & Trelford, 2003, p217.
[39] Ibid p230

between the bands, as Stiff Little Fingers were renowned for criticising both sides, while the republicanism of The O'Neil brothers continued to grow and be given expression (see in particular their post Undertones band 'That Petrol Emotion'[40]).

Furthermore, there was often dissent and disagreement on who was actually considered inside the imagined community. For example, there was a strong rejection of the Boomtown Rats as punk in any way.[41] A number of interviewees described them as "plastic punks" or as having "fake anger with one eye firmly on the money" (Dylan 15 July 2010), most, however, reserved their ire for their name. A large number of interviewees raised this, but I have selected Phil's quote for succinctness.

Boomtown fucking Rats, I don't think so. Do you know what Boomtown meant?

Interviewer: yeah Belfast

Right, exactly, it was Belfast, cause of the fucking bombs, you know [shouts] Boom, Boomtown and they took it as their name! Trying to claim the troubles as their own when it barely affected them. Hated them. Just using the name, it's like trying to say we are a part of you, we suffer alongside you, we are part of your community. No you're fucking not mate, piss right off. (Phil 27July 2011)

There is a duality to the Northern Irish punk community, which arises from its very nature as an imagined community within a society struggling over the issues of nationalism.[42] The dual nature is that it is open to all as befits the diy ethos, and yet it judges those who join and erects barriers to those it deems unsuitable or undesirable. In their attempt to create the community they want or need, they often present a closed or rigid appearance and boundary to those who are not a part of their imagined community. In other words, it was an evolving, mutating lived experience intertwined with a lived idea that continues to develop and engage new people whose experience of Northern Ireland will hopefully be very different from that of those featured in this chapter, and thus they will become responsible for a new punk community, which I look forward to seeing.

---

[40] There 1987 single 'Big Decision' (Polydor Records) contained text on the back sleeve decrying the use of plastic bullets by the RUC and the army, it does not fully acknowledge that they are the alternative to live rounds.

[41] http://starling.rinet.ru/music/temp/boomtownrats.html (last accessed 02.01.14) In the interests of balance this is a link to an extended interview with Bob Geldof in which he discusses his music in relation to the early punk scenes. http://www.amen.ie/articles/geldof.pdf

[42] There is a further, and more involved issue of nationalism in relation to Irish identity that has not been dealt with in this chapter as it is too involved a topic and should be engaged with on its own merits and discussions elsewhere. This is the problems created by The Pogues lyrics for those who lived outside of Ireland (typically England or America) but considered themselves Irish through their ancestral links and looked to understand the conflict through that lens. The Pogues presented a very specific form of Irish nationalism and republicanism that was often misunderstood or misinterpreted or deliberately left vague by the songwriters, but often those listening did not even realise that Ireland and Northern Ireland are two different countries. Consequently they (the listeners) had little impact on the Northern Irish punk scene so I choose not to engage with that issue in this chapter.

Concluding comments

The purpose of this chapter has not been to go through the bands that form, or formed, the Northern Irish punk scene, that has already been done expertly before by Glasper, O'Neil and Trelford. Indeed there are a number of websites continuing to fulfil this role such as http://nipunk.weebly.com/ and http://www.spitrecords.co.uk/bands.htm. Equally there are numerous personal and band based blogs one could turn to. Instead this chapter focused on demonstrating that within a fractured and unstable society at war with itself, punk was a means of bringing people together, enabling them to build up a community that was not based on division per se. However it was also important to acknowledge the division within the punk community, to realise its successes and its failure as no community is entirely one or the other.

Punks in Northern Ireland were the outsiders in many ways that punks on the mainland did not have to be, and could not conceive of being. They did not maintain the same divisions, the same entrenched partisan politics and ideologies as their parents, their communities and those in authority. Instead they willing wore the mantle of 'the other' in the hope of creating something new. It was not a great success, but sometimes a small step on the road can result in something unexpected and as I hope this chapter has demonstrated a great deal of fun can be had along the way.

Tearing at the flesh of decency

Original Artwork by Persons Unknown used in You're Already Dead by

A Flower in the Desert *Greg Bull*

Try again to capture and hold those happier times. A happy time. A good day to die or to remember. Sweet caresses and loving tender embrace. Sensual touch. Silk against my flesh. To put that longing away.

But here and now in this glorious sun. In the summertime of my late youth trying to imagine what it will be like to be old. To be thirty. No forty. No. Dead. Too much. Going too far. Burning up in this summer sun heat. I am here now and I do exist now and I am real now. More real than words. You read this and are here with me now. Forever now. Forever here and feeling what I feel. Like in a novel. Or a film. Reading this passage back over and over again. The endless scenes replaying as the flowers are washed away by the rain. Stood by the gate at the foot of the garden. Caressed by a beauty that burns from inside.

See?

So hard to think and make these thoughts into real words which make sense. My words come and go. More often than not. Sometimes struggling to find the correct word to fit the picture. Wonder what the stranger wants? Him all dressed in black. Watching. Been doing it for some time now. Weeks on and off. Months maybe before I noticed him.

And the messages coming to me from the news on TV. The voices calling me and whispering to me in the moments of quiet. Today so quiet. This one day alone. Like Dedalus. Wandering my own Odyssey. And still trying to. Pin. Down. That. One. Happy. Memory.

There are so many.

A single flower in the desert. Aylesbury Civic Arena. Awash with the debris of society. Youths. Pink hair. Red hair. Black hair. Dreadlocks. Mohicans. Shaved heads. Piercings and tattoos. Punks. Positive punks we/they were called. All waiting and watching. Nervous excited smiles. The air filled with the glory of electricity and tension and aggression. Electric atomic expectation. We all stared at the stage together. A coming together.

I am speeding out of my head. The pure adrenaline rush created by amphetamine sulphate snorted up in the toilets. Lucky I wasn't searched. Usually get a girl to smuggle it in or take it all before you get in to the gig. Expectation. Heart pounding fit to burst. Eyes wide. My eyes wide drinking it all in. The dark.

The movement of the crowd. The tidal wave of youth moving back and forth. Some shouts. Some guy with a huge Mohican is extorting the crowd. Trying to marshal them and lead them. His arms spread wide like he's being crucified. He laughs. Bare chested. Tribal tattoos cover his chest. Happy he turned back to the stage.

I stand and wait. Glued to the stage. I am keen to get started. The speed is making me fidgety and nervous. Keen to get on with it. The two pints of lager just enough to take the edge off and give me a buzz. But still I want to see and hear them.

The lights dimming. The backdrops. A slight hum from the PA and then it all goes dark and the hush really does fall over the crowd. A few whispered voices. The odd laugh. The bodies of the tribe are preparing themselves. Some turn and look around them seeking something. Looking for old faces and old friends. There are no battery humans here. I inhale. Breathe this in. The mix of sweat. Patchouli. Hashish. Alcohol. Perfume. Mostly a male dominated dancing space. Some of the older, seasoned punks gather at the front. Centre stage.

And now the ominous operatic music swells. That old tune from the Old Spice adverts. Carmen Burina or something. Never did bother to find out what it was called. Never cared enough. I just knew it meant they were coming. And there I stood rooted to the spot. Eyes wide. Speeding out of my head. Heart pumping. Waiting. Looking to the stage. Fidgeting. Leg twitching.

Then the crowd roar. And truly a Southern Death Cult walk onto the stage into the light. Alive with raw energy. A tribal trance. A ceremony. And did we worship? I think I did. I think I drank it all in. Standing there. Absorbing the moment. Were we all worshippers? Or is that just too romantic?

This was the New Church. This was the New Cathedral of Punk. Out of the rotting and stagnant corpse of 1977 the new naughty children were playing their new punk rock music. And we danced. Oh how we danced. And whirled. Like dervishes truly. Not an exaggeration to say we heaved and pulsed and writhed en masse. One giant human machine. We strutted. Yes like peacocks. Yes it's a cliché. And we all suddenly somehow believed it was all going to be ok.

And here in front of us was a man with a vision. And he was so filled with his hate and pent up aggression. He moved like a dancer across the stage. Face painted in his tribal colours and markings. Half red. Half white? Not sure I remember. Not much but his burning eyes. He was the new Jim Morrison. A new Johnny Lydon? No. So much more than that. The sneer on his lips at times. Leading us in a new Lord's Prayer. We swayed and we sang along. Chanted. We danced and we held onto something. This church was filled with acolytes. And we danced. Sweat dripping from my body. My t-shirt drenched. Soaked. Sweat and heat. Leather jackets. Studs. Did we all pray at this ceremony looking for new gods? I was certainly swept away as the music washed over me. Rising and lifting guitars. Brooding thundering bass. Tribal pounding drums. So sweet. Such sweet communion. Sinking and falling into a kind of bliss at that moment.

That singular moment in time.

My time in my memory.

So far away now.

Extract from <u>Perdam Babylonis Nomen</u> by Gregory Bull

Steve Ignorant – Crass – by Jacky Smith

The Political Pioneers of Punk (just don't mention the f-word!) *Helen Reddington*

Writing about punk has always been a risky business, especially when one is approaching from an academic perspective. Punk is anti-academic, and supposedly anti-formal; it prioritises the lived experience over both scholarly theory and mediated opinion. I will write more later in this chapter of the importance of being real as opposed to following theoretical directions, both in the living of a subcultural life itself and also in the approach to writing history.

It is a complicated path one must follow in order to negotiate potential accusations of hypocrisy in one's writing. Indeed, Furness notes the irritation expressed by Penny Rimbaud, initiator of the Crass collective, at the *No Future* punk conference organized by David Muggleton in 2001. Rimbaud declared the concept of a scholarly approach to punk as 'absurd… academics sitting round talking about something so anti-academic' (in Furness, 2012,15). I was there, having overcome my own misgivings about exactly the same issue, but found the conference to be hilariously affirming. As far as I know, Rimbaud didn't actually attend any of the sessions where academics supposedly sat round 'talking about something so anti-academic', but he did attend to make his own keynote speech, alongside Caroline Coon and Gary Valentine. Both he and Caroline were remarkably helpful to me as I sought to find women to interview for the book I later published. So this chapter is written with the awareness that (after McRobbie, 1990) firstly, I am a subjective writer, and secondly, that there are those who believe that anarchic music making should be excluded from academic discourse. Furness, of course, robustly defends those of us in particular that were actively engaged with punk as musicians during the 1970s and who now find ourselves as lecturers and researchers from a destination we had never envisaged, Higher Education.

From this position we have been able to insert our empirical experiences into more high-falutin' historical discourses, sometimes interrupting their flow with an insistence on revision based on our own experience of participation in a multi-stranded subculture; in my own case, this meant collecting the experiences of women who played rock instruments in punk bands and beginning to contextualize these within the greater punk, gender, political and historical discourses.

There are several reasons for writing this paper; in my earlier research, I was aware that I could only scratch the surface of the areas of punk and women's music-making that I was investigating; I had not documented the actual music (see forthcoming work, 2014), I had not addressed race or LGBT issues, and I had not explored the connection between the women in anarcho punk bands and feminism. Here, I hope to begin to discuss the importance of the women musicians of anarcho punk and the way their feminism was and is embedded within their musical praxis.

The women in punk were visible and vocal, making their presence felt on the street, as artists (Vivienne Westwood, Gee Vaucher, Linder Sterling), and as writers (Julie Burchill, Lucy Toothpaste) as well as musicians. This was of great importance: they were audible for the first time as rock beings, not only following in the footsteps of 'hollerers' like Janis Joplin, Tina Turner and the other strong female vocal role models that had come before them, but also appearing on stage playing electric guitars, electric basses, drums and keyboards and making 'boy-noise', redefining it as aesthetically and technically their own. I will examine in greater detail a subculture within a subculture: the explicitly pacifist and feminist (amongst many other things) subgenre of anarcho punk, which stubbornly celebrated its subculture-ness even as the Birmingham School definitions of subcultures began to be deconstructed with the onset of Thatcherism and the beginnings of the 20th century fin-de-siecle philosophy, postmodernism. I will be focusing on the period in the UK between roughly 1978 and 1984; this is because during this period the political changes in the British social landscape were tumultuous and made a transition from entropy to proactive monetarism, and the most influential of the anarcho punk bands, Crass, dissolved in 1984.

Moral Authority and Punk Subcultural Authenticity: a context

The Sex Pistols had articulated an ennui and frustration felt by an angry generation parented by men and women who had experienced the horrors of the Second World War and the subsequent boom of 1960s Britain and who did not want to accept the rules and regulations of that decade that had no relevance to their world of strikes and unemployment.

Johnny Rotten's 'moral authority' (York, 1980, 48) was a strong foil for the hypocritical moral stance of the mainstream British media, which was intent on demonizing the current generation of young people. Hebdige describes the historic friction between the mainstream and perceived threats to established culture, citing Williams' 'aesthetic and moral criteria for distinguishing the worthwhile products from the "trash"' (1979, 8), the 'moral conviction' of Barthes' beliefs (ibid, 10) and Gramsci's critique of the social authority of the mainstream (ibid, 16). It is no wonder that punk, with its celebration of its own trash aesthetic, excited academia. The hippy project had apparently failed, its alternative approach quickly appearing to become commercialized and its libertarian politics leading to, for instance, the Oz trial that revealed a darker side to the peace and free love message[43]

Johnny Rotten was savvy enough to abandon punk just as it was being consolidated and fought over but he and others who instigated the phenomenon left a powerful legacy. The pace at which groups of people became active musicians, and their self-definition as punks, indicates that the idea of anarchy (however presented) functioned effectively as the last-ditch solution for young people who desperately needed a sense of agency in their lives. In addition, the UK pub rock and folk scenes had been thriving during this period, effectively reserving and preparing entry-level venues for the sudden influx of usually younger, angrier bands and artists. The Sex Pistols had shown people that it could be done and from that point onwards the actual content of the music and lyrics became unique to each band.

This was exciting- and musicians such as those who formed The Clash soon crossed over from their rock beginnings into punk, where they could incorporate reggae ideas and political sloganeering into music that further articulated the 'now' that was being experienced by the young generation.

Both bands' reputations grew to the extent that first The Sex Pistols and then The Clash (in 1977) signed to major labels, thus arguably becoming part of the machine that they had been raging against. Suddenly, The Clash seemed more akin to normal rock artists; they had sold rebellion as just another commodity. Some fans were aghast whereas others followed dutifully, enjoying the musical development of the Clash and mourning the eventual demise of the Sex Pistols. Clark summarises the odd polarity that had happened: '… when the mainstream proved that it needed punk, punk's equation was reversed: its negativity became positively commercial' (2003,233). Hebdige enlarges on this recuperation process and quotes Sir John Read, then Chairman of EMI, who was delighted that money appeared to be more important than the message to a selection of traditional 'brilliant nonconformists' (Hebdige's words, op cit. 99)) who 'became in the fullness of time, wholly acceptable and can (sic) contribute greatly to the development of modern music' (ibid, 99). Poison Girls' 1984 lyric: 'Made a bomb out of music/ Made a hit with a record' could not have been more apt ('Take the Toys', 1984).

---

[43] Despite this, Geoff Travis (who set up Rough Trade and The Cartel which distributed punk records all over the UK and Europe), Penny Rimbaud and many more who formed the framework for branches of punk and post-punk activity were firmly rooted in hippy ideals and aesthetics.

However, the 'selling out' and consequent opportunity to communicate challenges to the opinions of a wider audience had a positive effect, according to Laing:

> ... the example of The Clash in developing a dialect of political comment within the rock mainstream should not be underestimated. Without that example (as well as punk's general impact) it is unlikely that the songs ofUB40 and of 'Two Tone' groups like The Specials would have found the general popularity they enjoyed from 1979 onwards' (1985,117)

Even Cogan, who dismisses the politics of The Clash as 'vague political leanings', admits that...'the more commercialized bands could be seen as a gateway to the more ideologically involved bands' (2007, 87). As it became apparent, however, that being in a punk band could set musicians en route to becoming mainstream, the Clash template (a rock band becomes a punk band becomes a rock band again) began to function for other artists. Moral authority passed on to those punks who embedded moral issues into their music and who eschewed commercialization by taking on board the *idea* of anarchy espoused by The Sex Pistols and the overt political sloganeering of The Clash, but opted out of the drive to become wealthy.

It is in the nature of innovative creative activities that as they become more widespread, and inspirational beyond their central core, new 'rules' are created, and ironically the group of people who created anarcho punk, Crass, as an authentic political resistance to the commercialization of the music genre spawned a style template of their own. Allan Whalley from Chumbawumba observed much later on: '... it quickly became obvious that they were setting up a kind of blueprint, and a lot of people just followed that blueprint blindly'.(Glasper, 2006, 379). This contributed to a conflict within the greater punk community itself about exactly what punk was; was it a London-centric fashion phenomenon based on Chelsea's King's Road, that finished almost as soon as it started; or was it intended as a blueprint for subcultural activities in hotspots all over the UK? Was it a return to working class roots (the journalist Gary Bushell's 'Oi' vision, was it a corruptible concept that exposed weaknesses in the British Record Industry (Savage, 1991), or was it the missing link between politics and music making for a dispossessed generation? In reality, it could be any of these things; as Laing says above, the environment created by even those bands that had 'sold out' enabled those who were more purist or even obscurantist to thrive. Lyrically, the concerns of a generation were being expressed; sonically, the intention was still to assault the mainstream aesthetic. To those outside the subculture, it probably all sounded the same; to those within it, it was nuanced by a multitude of delineations.

Authentic anger

Nehring cites Bakhtin, Benjamin and Brecht) as being '… quite specific about which emotion is most vital: anger resentful of injustice.' (1997,136). He notes that the concept of postmodernism that was so popular at the time of writing in the later years of the 20th century aimed to downplay the emotions, and thus challenged the core of authenticity. Authenticity itself is a constantly shifting concept; Moore writes of:

> …a globalising perspective… that artists speak the truth of their own situation; that they speak the truth of the situation of (absent) others; and that they speak the truth of their own culture, thereby representing (present) others. (2002, 209)

And later of the change in academic perspective, the

> … shift from consideration of the intention of various originators towards the activities of various perceivers, and should focus on the reasons they might have for finding, or failing to find, a particular performance authentic. (2002, 221)

Postmodernism, with its focus on the crisis of proliferation, developed as a philosophy just at the point in time when philosophy should have engaged with feminism; it has questioned the way we relate to history. Nehring says that emotion is vital to processing social and cultural situations and understanding them:

> Since the eighteenth century and the birth of aesthetics (or the philosophy of art), academics and other intellectuals have held that meaningless emotional appeals are characteristic of the low or popular arts produced by the marketplace' (ibid, xi)

The punks who became involved with anarcho punk were looking for truth, and the anger expressed in the music affirmed for them the sincerity of the bands; this anger was not always a force for positivity, however. McKay writes of the way that '… subcultural energy can divert itself from… the constructively utopian to the simply self-destructive' (1996,28). Subcultural divisions are emphasized by 'musical and generational differences' (ibid, 29). So subcultural music makers need to be wary about their own disdain for other forms of street music: the competition within and between the taste cultures present (Gans, 1999) in the youth field risks dismissing the emotions attached to genres of music that they do not subscribe to, and thus dismisses the subsequent power of those emotions as agents for change. Rather than the basic message that inspired it, this internal friction can become the focus of a youth movement, especially at the margins of music making.

With regard to women in bands, their active engagement in music making alongside male peers, their *being punks* through *doing the music,* and their visibility were factors that consolidated a realist feminism at the time, far from theoretical discourses that sought to ignore the lived experiences of women by setting their sights on grander and more abstract horizons; it appeared to be natural, which was one of its strengths. Crass, or specifically Penny Rimbaud, had made a transition from the hippy subculture and its free festival ethos into punk; this development included many of the principles of access and sharing that had been articulated in, for instance, the free festival movement in Britain which gained momentum after the first Glastonbury Fayre in 1971 led to free festivals at Windsor and Stonehenge in following years (see McKay, 1996). The emphasis was on independence from mainstream social and political structures; as Dunn, who documents contemporary anarcho punk, notes of Crass: 'While other bands and activists in the punk scene paid lip service to the concept of self-reliance, Crass made it a touchstone of their daily lives' (Dunn, 2012, 203)

Anarchy

Because punk, unlike previous British subcultures, had the creation music at its heart from the outset, it had developed 'inescapable links' with the music industry, as Laing remarks. It had begun as an

> ... outlawed shadow of the music industry and its fate depended equally on the
> response to it of the industry. And while punk as a life-style developed a certain distance
> from the fate of punk rock, it remained dependent on the existence of a musical focus
> to give its own identity a stability. (Laing, 1985:xi)

Disentangling these links and putting an alternative in place was an act of great ambition Zillah describes the first contact she had with the collective at a gig with UK Subs at The crypt at North East London Polytechnic:

> That's where I first met them. They were there in the audience talking to people, which was really different. Not only were they in the audience, they were sharing. So if you got there earlier and they were having a cup of tea, they would ask you if they wanted a cup of tea. They weren't being a 'famous band'. They were being part of the audience and part of the whole experience.

The anarchy practiced by Crass was connected to European underground politics and in London they aligned themselves with political centres such as the Centro Iberico in west London that hosted Spanish anarchists from the Basque country:

> I knew it was political... the police kept turning up and having fights with everybody, along with the Skinheads, and the Skinheads would object to what they were saying. And also Crass were known for playing strange places like the Anarchy Centres. So that's where we knew that the anarchy thing was happening. The difference was that people were actively being political, using anarchy as the framework. We took it as meaning 'do what you want' as well[44].

Uniformity

The anarcho punk bands struggled with the way that they presented their ideas; as McKay writes, their '...utopian politics [is] presented through dystopian cultural formations' (1996,89) and in their constant questioning of the status quo struggled against a phenomenon articulated by Plant:

> Questions of where the revolution comes from must be joined by those which reveal the means by which revolutions are betrayed, an interrogation which might suggest that remnants of counter-revolutionary desire are invested in even the most radical of gestures (1992:123)

Artists are often pursued by their own desire for the safety of consolidation, and petrified into stasis by being defined by pronouncements they make and activities they undertake that were originally intended to be fluid or transient. Radical art is terrifying and dangerous; a world without boundaries is much more difficult to negotiate than one with obvious and distasteful political, commercial and social parameters. The brand of anarchy practiced by Crass encouraged bands that were associated with them (mainly by playing gigs with them but also for some, recording on their self-titled label) to define themselves any way they wanted to. Unfortunately, the 'blueprint' identified earlier by Chumbawumba's Whalley became a default setting for some of the bands who were originally inspired by Crass. Indeed, Kay Byatt from Youth in Asia remarks that although she remains committed right to the present day to the same non-conformist causes that she wrote lyrics about while an active band member, she eventually left the group because 'punk's formality' started to tire her:

> [I had] thought the scene was about breaking rules, not making them. It became a very 'right on' movement, and maybe a little too puritanical for its own good, with Crass looked upon as virtual gods towards the end (ibid, 164)

---

[44] It should not be forgotten that both Ana Da Silva, guitarist in the Raincoats, had become politicized in her native Portugal, and Palmolive, who drummed for both The Slits and The Raincoats, hailed from Spain, where in 1975 Franco's death led to the gradual introduction of democracy through a difficult transition period. This is not to say that all of the women who played in punk bands were overtly politically active; it is undeniable, however, that amongst some of them there was a level of political consciousness that may have set them apart from their peers.

The bleakness of Crass's garb had practicality at its heart, claims Zillah:

> That's what happens, I think- you start off with all the interesting, arty people and by arty people I mean people who do stuff for themselves, not necessarily art college, just people with imagination, and then as things get popular everyone seems to think they've got to join in with the popular look rather than their individual look. The whole Crass thing: they (the audience) all started dressing in black, they all had to have their hair a certain way, and for the macho bit what happened really was not that the people within the anarchy scene that got macho, it was the opposition that came. The skinheads that came to beat you up, the normal people that came to beat you up. I think that got really scary and therefore the men and women in that scene would start to wear their Doctor Martins in case they had to have a fight, their black trousers in case they had to hide. People toned it down a bit more, wanted to hide a bit more.

This was also affirmed by Vi Subversa, who cited the need to wear 'fairly armoured clothes to feel safe' (in Steward and Garratt,1984,37); regardless of her comments above, Rubella Ballet dressed in day-glo colours, Indeed, Steve Ignorant himself refers to Rubella Ballet's colourful rule-breaking as 'a breath of fresh air', a change from the uniformly dour and black-clad presentation that was favoured by Crass and other bands within the genre. (Glasper, 58).

Rubella Ballet's colour was an exception. In general, anarcho punks rejected camp, for as Sontag says, 'To emphasize style is to slight content' (1982, 107). The first wave of punk had layers of irony throughout it, and could be read as purely style (hence Hebdige's focus). Those who historicize punk as following on from David Bowie's short-haired glam image rightly saw a camp androgyny embedded within it, and this was simple to read. The black 'pervy' clothing and the slogans were easy to recuperate and commodify. This rapid absorbtion into the world of fashion threatened the validity of punk and contributed to the many heated authenticity debates of the time.

The Female Presence in Anarcho Punk Bands

Although creating an all-female rock band was arguably a radical political act in itself[45] some of the male punks found this idea difficult to engage with; being an 'out' feminist could be seen as a risky option (see Reddington, 2012, 182-189). Isolated from each other largely by a 1970s ideology that can be explained by reference to Potter's writing about tokenism (1997) many of the female punk groups at the time

---

[45] this would possibly come as a surprise to all-female German skiffle band 'Lucky Girls' and British 1960s garage band 'Mandy and the Girlfriends, see von der Grun, 1983, 41, and Phillips and Brown, 2012),

were regarded by the media as competitors (Gina Birch in Reddington, op cit. 188), although in reality their personnel had often collaborated musically in different configurations before their bands consolidated and made recordings. There had been reluctance amongst some of the first-wave female punk bands, especially The Slits, to identify themselves as feminists, much to early manager Caroline Coon's frustration (Caroline Coon in Reddington, op cit 183). In the music that emanated from Britain's Women's Centres during the mid-1970s, feminism could be regarded as of equal importance to the music that was created[46]. Within the anarcho punk movement that consolidated towards 1980, feminism was often integrated into the ethos of the bands, as part of the general force for change that was expressed in the lyrics; these lyrics explored themes of pacifism, vegetarianism, revolution, and acceptance of queerness (the A-heads' *Isolated*) amongst other issues[47]. This willingness to engage directly with feminism set the anarcho bands apart from some of the more feted women in punk bands. There were many bands under this umbrella that had female members; these included Dirt, Lost Cherrees, and Hagar the Womb; I have chosen here to focus mainly on Poison Girls (originally formed in Brighton and later, based in Epping) Rubella Ballet (sometimes also labeled 'Positive Punks' because of their colourful visuals) and Crass. Poison Girls were particularly influential on feminist discourse and practice in anarcho punk bands, partly because they were active from a relatively early date (1977) and toured with Crass from 1979 onwards building an audience alongside them. They introduced feminist ideas to, for instance, Dirt (Glasper, 2006, 60) who say they were inspired by them and other female-fronted bands; Youth in Asia, who celebrated their own 50/50 gender split (ibid, 160) and who also cite Crass as an inspiration; and Flowers in the Dustbin, who also cite Patti Smith as being influential (ibid, 171 and see Whiteley, 2000).

In anarcho punk bands there appears to have been little fear from either male or female personnel of identifying with feminist politics. Steve Battershill, a founder member of Lost Cherrees (who started in 1981), recalls:

> The feminist stance (sic) was struck very early on and has never wavered; equality in all walks of life is essential to us. The issue had already been raised by Crass and Poison Girls, so, although it wasn't that widespread, people were starting to seriously address such problems' (in Glasper, 2006, 149)

---

[46] More details about this can be found at http://womensliberationmusicarchive.co.uk/

[47] The free speech encouraged by the movement also led to some unfortunate pronouncements such as those made by Admit You're Shit's John Cato, who aligned his views with the racist British Movement. (Glasper, 2006, 120); most anarcho punk bands were anti-racist, although in common with other punk bands, predominantly consisting of white people.

Between them, Poison Girls, Rubella Ballet and Crass covered a broad area of feminist music making and performed to mixed audiences in a distinctive subcultural area carved out by the activities of Crass themselves, although both Rubella Ballet and Poison Girls had originally formed as a result of the catalyst effect of earlier punk activity in the UK. A feeling of agency was a vital element in the development of the genre as a whole. As Zillah Minx, founder member of Rubella Ballet says that in spite of the idea of anarchy being introduced by the Sex Pistols, the political application came later:

> I believed I was part of the whole creating of punk. The music then was what was being created by artistic people to do whatever they thought was weird and different. It wasn't until Crass came along that it seemed [overtly] political. Previous to that the Sex Pistols and X Ray Spex didn't seem anarchist [in the way they behaved]. We looked up the word anarchy, and that started to make us think politically.[48]

Participation in the 'creating of punk' was something that many young (and older) people felt had been an important role, even before punk was actually named. Shanne Bradley, the bass player from the punk band The Nips, remarks:

> I was around in '75 at St Albans. The Pistols played there. That's how I got drawn into the whole thing. It wasn't called Punk. We were wearing the same sort of thing; I had short spiky hair after a peroxide accident with henna, and a lot of piercings, and holsters and ripped up fishnets and ice-skating boots and stuff from Oxfam shops.[49]

This shows that punk felt to some of its original protagonists as if it was inevitable, a gathering of people and a common mindset. The music and atmosphere at live gigs continued to strike a chord long after punk's first burst of activity in west London had died away. Eve Libertine describes visiting the Crass house (Dial House in Epping) after being so 'moved by the raw energy' of their performances that she would sometimes be the only audience member left at the gig, as the band emptied venues with their uncompromising sound. She describes her feeling that '...there was a rather one-dimensional quality to what was then an all-male outfit- the onstage politics lacked a feminist angle, a problem that was easily solved by Joy and myself joining the band'. (interview in Raha, 2005, 94). Crass then embedded feminism into their ethos, according to Joy De Vivre, who was able to state that: 'It is not easy to isolate feminist activities of the band, they're so tied in with the wider philosophy about compassion, respect, pacifism'. (ibid, 94). The 1981 Crass album *Penis Envy* epitomizes the willingness of the collective to invest time and energy into a specifically feminist approach to the art of making music. Prior to this,

---

[48] Interview with author date
[49] Interview with author date

Raha describes de Vivre's song-poem *Women* as being related from a 'nonacademic perspective' and thus appealing to everywoman (and man) (ibid, 95).

This simplicity of expression was also embedded into male members of the anarcho-punk musical community: hence Crass group member Steve Ignorant's name: he was, he says 'ignorant of politics' (ibid,23) when he first came to the collective. Delivering a direct anti-sexist message alongside the other concerns associated with anarcho punk meant that the message was validated and communicated in a simple and uncompromising way, at a great distance from theoretical feminism that many of the protagonists in the subculture might have found indigestible or possibly even hostile. One of Crass' s more high profile pranks involved the duping of 'teeny romance' magazine *Loving* into releasing a white vinyl version of their track *Our Wedding*, which had been created in a spirit of sarcasm. Once the hoax had been discovered, the News of the World presented it as 'Band of Hate's Loving Message', quoting the obviously distressed editor of *Loving,* Pam Lyons, response to the 'sick joke' (Penny Rimbaud, 2009, in sleeve-notes to *Penis Envy*). Whether this was a feminist act or an act of misogyny is debatable; feminism involves choices and freedoms that are surely espoused by anarchists. It is possible that a teenage girl (especially during the dour 1970s) is entitled to dream about whatever she wants to (see Walkerdine, 1997), even if an anarchist collective consisting of an older generation deeply disapproves. This type of cross-generational friction continues to happen to the present day, with every party feeling that the other is simultaneously manipulated and manipulative, and at the time of writing is being played out predominantly in a relationship between the mainstream pop music industry , pornography and shock tactics ; oddly enough, this looks to the deviation popularized by the original London punks as an inspiration, as Linder Sterling could attest after seeing Lady Gaga's Meat Dress. However, in one (often unacknowledged) area, the anarchism of punk, and in particular, that of anarcho punk, 'worked': the passing on of skills and learning to peers.

Apprenticeships and Mentoring

As well as a sort of off-piste social and political education, the anarcho-punk groups fostered the same informal musical mentoring that was essentially a concentrated and accelerated version of the way that popular musicians were learning in the world outside punk. This was also common in feminist music making circles (Bayton, 1998,72)

This freedom was not as easily acquired or defined as it might have looked from the outside, and for instance in Brighton it took the music-making an older woman, Vi Subversa from Poison Girls, to pioneer the odd blend of hippy and punk ideals that developed into anarcho-punk's feminist musical agenda. In Brighton's local music scene Vi was mentor to many of the up-and-coming bands, helping to infuse their music with political consciousness, later relocating to Essex and collaborating with Crass. Her earlier involvement with the music for the 1975 theatrical production The Body Show led to a musical nucleus that included female bass-player Bella Donna, a friend of The Buzzcocks. Vi had been proactive in setting up a ramshackle rehearsal complex in the cellars of a Presbyterian Church in North Road in Brighton.. This involved sitting on the management committee of a community group that involved Church Elders, '...and because I was middle-aged, they trusted me'[50]. Poison Girls went on to lend equipment and even band members to start-up bands in the Brighton punk scene that subsequently developed, giving support and encouragement to scores of bands. [51]The facilitation of music making by lending equipment and other forms of support was inherent to punk and was a major catalyst for encouraging people to perform who could not have done so otherwise; it had this in common with feminist music circles of the time (ibid, 1998,72) but also with the much more popular stream of punk music; Siouxsie and the Banshees, for instance, borrowed equipment from Johnny Thunders and the Heartbreakers.

Meanwhile, Crass in turn were creating a politically active framework-by-example for the punks around them who were disappointed by what they saw as the petering out of the energy associated with the first burst of energy that the Sex Pistols had instigated. As Zillah remarks: 'We were all really gutted when the Sex Pistols split up. We wanted everyone to think our way'.

Zillah cites Crass as showing her contemporaries 'how to *live* as anarchy', even if she and the other members of Rubella Ballet rejected the polemic and harsh visual style of their friends. Crass redefined their corner of punk as a medium for practicing ideas of a different way of being, which included a critique on gender politics. The open-mindedness of the collective allowed them to examine gender roles to a point as we have seen, although within the nucleus of the collective itself, it was still the women who sang and the men who (mostly) played the loud instruments; anarcho punk was not always a site of equality; in London, the band Hagar the Womb were founded after: '...finding it hard to get

---

[50] Letter to author, 2000
[51] The extent of the activity centred around The Vault as a rehearsal and gigging space, and its significance to the Brighton Punk Scene can be seen at www.punkbrighton.co.uk, the website set up by ex-punk Phil Byford to archive the Brighton bands.

ourselves heard or involved in any sense. Anarchy in Wapping or no, the battle of the sexes continues...' As Ruth Elias, founder member of the female-dominated band, says, '"Pre Crass-invasion" the Wapping Anarchy Centre had been male-dominated, and out of anger, [our] 'band of defiance' was set up to give women from the Centre a chance to participate actively in the scene (in Glasper, 154-155).

Women in marginal political groupings had often found themselves in the position of handmaidens to the folk heroes, without agency and operating as a mirror image of those in the world outside their political sphere. This phenomenon was clearly articulated by Rowbotham in 1973, and has still not really been successfully counteracted in the present day, which is why the Pussy Riot Collective has had such a strong impact.

Anarcho punk, loosely defined as it was, embedded into practice the mentoring of up and coming punk bands, with integrated female personnel, and the facilitation of gigs and events for those bands to perform at. From Mark Perry's original instruction 'This is a chord, This is another, This is a third, Now form a band' (Mark P in Savage, 1991) to the sleeve notes on the Desperate Bicycles 1977 single *The medium was tedium b/w Don't back the Front*, 'It was easy, it was cheap, go and do it', there was a clearly-defined articulation of do-it-yourself empowerment that was not restricted to man-to-man peer learning, and in this respect anarcho punk followed general punk musical practice.

Vi Subversa; a pioneering personality

Fronting the band Poison Girls at the age of 40, Vi was an older woman and a mother in a scene that was predominantly (although not exclusively) youth-based. If Vi felt that she could stand in front of an audience with a guitar and sing punk songs with her band, so should anyone else; the enabling factors of her example should not be underestimated. The punk women who took to the stage were pioneers of their time (I have explored this in depth, Reddington 2012) but in respect of being an older woman, Vi's pioneering activity was doubly inspiring. She challenged not only gender assumptions, but also assumptions about what a middle-aged parent ought to be doing, and thus caused many young male punks to question many more of their attitudes than simply those associated with the 'fun' aspect of punk. Unlike the Mom-rockers of Middle America (see Coates 87-101, in Jennings and Gardner, 2012), Vi was overtly political and fully understood the implications of living what was essentially a rock'n'roll lifestyle with her family both in tow and actively engaged in live events. As Bayton notes, Vi, with her daughter playing beside her, could inspire a three year old girl to want to play guitar in a band, and was one of the many '... women that I interviewed [who] were highly aware that they... were serving as role models for other women'. In response, Vi remarked: 'I feel really privileged to be part of that'. (Bayton, 1990:62)[52]

During her years in Poison Girls Vi was the embodiment of difference, the proof that subversion was happening and that the world that the young punks lived in was challengeable and could look very different. This type of discursive production put issues of performativity (Butler, 1990) at the heart of the main stream of anarcho punk, during the time that Poison Girls toured with Crass.

Zillah Ashworth: apprenticeships

Zillah's approach to Rubella Ballet, supported by her partner Sid, was to encourage novice female instrumentalists to join the band and learn their playing skills onstage. From female bass-player Gemma (Vi's daughter), who started with the band, she later employed her sister and other female players. 'I thought it made a statement', said Zillah,

> I wanted as many girls as possible and sometimes that didn't really help when the girls weren't very good as musicians because they hadn't had the experience that the men had had. It was different for them as well, being that forward on bass at gigs with blokes jumping on you or spitting at you or whatever.

Later on, the band employed a very skilled young musician:

> ...Leda Baker, who was Ginger Baker's daughter, she'd been to one of our gigs and someone mentioned to her that we were looking for a guitarist; when she rang up and said that she was interested in coming over, I was thrilled, I thought, 'A girl guitarist, brilliant!' and when she came over, I couldn't believe it- she played like Jimi Hendrix. We didn't know who she was; and it was some time before she told us who her dad was. We couldn't believe it but it sort of went with what she was playing. And she was only 18.

---

[52] Poison Girls lent me a bass guitar and lent my band a drummer, Vi's 14-year-old son Danny, for our first few gigs in Brighton.

Fluidity of line-up was part of the ethos of Rubella Ballet, who had no expectations of formal relationships with their personnel; because Zillah had been very taken by the fact that at an early Crass gig, the band had mingled with the audience and made them cups of tea:

> With Rubella Ballet there was this whole thing of 'singers in and out, bass players in and out', so it was very fluid, who was playing what and who was singing what so for the first half dozen gigs there was different people in the band. Like the band being in the audience!

Re-branding History: feminism versus postmodernism

The feminist writer MacKinnon had in the 1970s 'imagined that feminists would retheorise life in the concrete rather than spend the next three decades on metatheory, talking *about* theory, rehashing over and over in this disconnected way how theory should be done, leaving women's lives twisting in the wind'. (2000,25). The revision of the meaning of the punk subculture seen through decades polluted by the concept of postmodernism downplays the importance of the active role of women during the punk moment. After punk, as anarcho punk has widened its scope to a global perspective and slipped deeper underground only to materialize at Stop the City and other anti-capitalist events, the movement retains its gender awareness. Eve Libertine's arrival at the house in Epping had caused the musicians in the collective to incorporate a deconstructed approach to gender which remains in anarcho punk to this day, as Nicholas confirms:

> Anarcho-punks concerned with deconstructing gender engage in specifically *feminist* poststructuralist tactics, which work from the assumption of a historicised, reified gender order and evade a simplistic, voluntaristic solution.... These deconstructive readings are ensured either through the tactics of exaggeration or literalization or through the fostering of a critical framework of perception for scene participants (via the wider cultural creations of punk) to be able to read gendered acts ironically and anti-foundational. This fostering of modes of perception stay true to the DIY anarchist ethos of autonomy and remains non-coercive and non-authoritarian by making these tactics 'scrupulously visible', relying on participants' ethico-political choice that the post-gender ethos is indeed preferable. (Nicholas, 2007:18)

In this, contemporary anarcho punk arguably evades the fate of more (ironically) 'mainstream' subcultures; Clark writes that

> ...commodification and trivialization of subcultural style is becoming ever more rapid and, at the turn of the millennium, subcultures are losing certain powers of speech. Part of what has become the hegemonic discourse of subcultures is a misrepresentative depoliticization of subcultures; the notion that subcultures were and are little more than hairstyles, quaint slang, and pop songs. In the prism of nostalgia, the politics and ideologies of subcultures are often stripped from them. (2003, 231)

The re-branding of subcultures as *only* variations of style, recuperated in selective nostalgia and inauthenticated by default, has culminated in a sneering dismissal of youth culture by writers such as Heath and Potter, who in their 2005 book *The Rebel Sell* distil a rationale for capitalism as a logocentric ideal, and to some extent fulfill MacKinnon's fears about the legacy of postmodern philosophy. MacKinnon derides the way that postmodern theorists swerve around reality, dealing in 'factish things' (op cit. 17); their dismissal of social frameworks has retrospectively affected attitudes to the histories of young people, women and all those not in the hegemonic layers of society. If we refer to Plant's observation, it is possible that such writers often simply do not possess the radar that enables them to register subversive activity; she talks of the '...networks of subversion which continue to arise even on the most postmodern pockets of the postmodern world...' (1992,176). Plant continues: 'That a great deal of cultural agitation is hidden from the public gaze is sometimes indicative of its tactics rather than its absence.' (ibid). This was apparent in the way that Riot Grrrl functioned in the 1990s (see Leonard 2007, Monem, 2007 and others) .It is also entirely likely that in the 21st century, the public is simply gazing in the wrong direction, as Huq asserts (2006).

Looking back on punk, historians often struggle to define its meaning; Sabin discussed this problem as he tried to delineate the scope of his anthology on the cultural legacy of punk (1999, 4-6). As hard as it was to delineate at the time, it has been even harder to delineate in retrospect; it could seem destructive, but creativity was at its heart. Politically it was fluid and could/can appear to affirm whatever the writer or researcher looks for within it. In Young's utopian book, *Electric Eden*, he remarks that:

> "It's interesting to speculate what might have resulted had punk's musical cleansing spared some notion of folk- which was, after all, the culture of citizens, not aristocrats; a music for the leveled society... In Germany, France, Italy and elsewhere, punk was a way of life more associated with the peace movement, animal rights, squatting and environmentalism. In Britain, popular opinion was swift to cast such righteous communitarianism as the enemy within'. (2010, 535)[53]

We need to add feminism to Young's list; as citizens with no space for their voices to be heard except within the narrow parameters of mainstream stereotypes that so rapidly re-established themselves as punk's opportunities were replaced by Thatcher's enterprise culture. Women with power are

---

[53] According to Young, Crass were the only punk band to succeed in fusing the ethos of both, and he describes them as 'folk-punk-anarchist'. (ibid, 535). But the Raincoats were also labeled as punk folk music, largely due to their willingness to experiment with non-amplified instruments associated with non-Western cultures (Da Silva in von Burden, 2010, 102).

acknowledges as such only when they fit the template created by men with power, and are measured against it. As Nicholas writes:

> Particularly relevant to feminist ideas has been the notion that discourses constitute us and thus both enable and limit us through the subject positions they make available to us. Thus the limits of discourses within which subjects can 'be' represent the limits to subjects' agency. (2007, 4-5)

Feminism still operates in a limited environment. In parallel with the subculture of punk itself and matched against the affirmation of power of the mainstream that punk created by its very existence, feminism is and was necessary because misogyny and sexism exist; but just imagine what women could do with their energy if they were not expending time and energy being feminists. Resistance to male domination takes up space that could be used to better purposes; and because feminism has had as many definitions as punk has, the whole idea of 'fourth generation feminism' at the time of writing seems risible; a comment on the anarchist collective CrimethInc's blog, quoted by Nicholas, sums this up perfectly: 'Thus we find the ironic but coherent corollary in anarcho punk gender politics that 'feminists fight to put an end to gender' (op cit. Nicholas, 8). One of the struggles of feminism has been the impossibility of creating a shape that fits all women. Radstone talks of 'the void' as she attends a feminist conference in Glasgow in 1991 and becomes aware of the differences in articulation and experience between not only a very direct Women's Studies Network conference the weekend before and the Feminist Theory Conference at which she was presenting a paper, but also the 'tough journey from the Gorbals' described in the speech of welcome by the female Lord Provost of Glasgow (Radstone, 106 in Kemp and Squires, 1997,104-108). Gender discourse does not belong exclusively to anyone, but it appears that it can best be articulated and tested in the margins of politics and the academy.

It is my belief that one of the most powerful things we can do for our gender is to reinsert women into historical discourses and to understand the reasons for our omission. Nicholas (above) writes from the perspective of relatively contemporary anarcho punk feminism, still alive and well, but hidden. Documentation of the moment still emerges, gradually. Zillah's film 'She's a Punk Rocker' presents a series of very different women talking personally about the meaning of punk; documentaries such as hers facilitate a feeling of authenticity that captures a moment between the camera starting and the end of filming: her subjects (who include Gee and Eve Libertine from Crass, Poly Styrene from X-Ray

Spex, Gaye Black from The Adverts, Hagar the Womb and others, are talking to a friend who understands them as much as to a camera. The conversation will continue, and perhaps Crass will make the tea.

Bibliography

Bayton, Mavis (1998) *Frock Rock: Women Performing Popular Music* Oxford and New York: Oxford University Press

Burden, Zora von (2010) *Women of the Underground: Music. Cultural innovators speak for themselves* San Francisco: Manic D Press

Butler, Judith(1999) [1990]. *Gender Trouble: Feminism and the Subversion of Identity (Subversive bodily acts, IV Bodily Inscriptions, Performative Subversions)*. New York: Routledge

Clark, Dylan (2003) *The Death and Life of Punk, the Last Subculture*, in Muggleton, David and Weinzierl, Rupert (2003) *The Post-subcultures Reader* Oxford and New York: Berg
Pp 223-236

Cogan, Brian "Do They Owe Us a Living? Of Course They Do!" Crass, Throbbing Gristle, and Anarchy and Radicalism in Early English Punk Rock *Journal for the Study of Radicalism* Vol. 1, No. 2 (Summer 2007), pp. 77-90 Michigan State University Press accessed 29/1/114

Coates, Norma (2012) 'Mom Rock? Media Representations of 'Women Who Rock' in Jennings,R and Gardner, A (2012) *'Rock On': Women Ageing and Popular Music* Farnham and Burlington: Ashgate

Dunn, Kevin (2012) 'Anarcho Punk and Resistance in Everyday Life' *Punk and Post Punk* 1:2, pp201-218

Furness, Zak (2012) *Punkademics: the basement show in the ivory tower* Wivenhoe/Brooklyn/Port Watson: Minor Compositions

Frith, Simon and Goodwin, Andrew (eds) (1998) *On Record: rock, pop and the written word* London and New York: Routledge

Gans, Herbert (1999) *Popular Culture and High Culture: an analysis and evaluation of taste* New York: Basic Books

Gosling, Tim (2004) '"Not for Sale": The Underground Network of Anarcho-Punk' in Bennett, Andy, and Peterson, Richard A. *Music Scenes: Local, Translocal and Virtual*. (168-186) Vanderbilt University Press

Glasper, Ian (2006) *The Day the Country Died: a history of anarcho punk 1980-1984* London: Cherry Red

Grun, Rita von der (1983) *Venus Weltklang: Musikfrauen- Frauenmusik* Berlin:Elefanten

Heath, J. and Potter, A., (2005). *The Rebel Sell. How the counterculture became consumer culture*. Chichester, West Sussex: Capstone

Hebdige, Dick (1979) *Subculture, the Meaning of Style* London:Methuen

Huq, Rupa (2006) Beyond Subculture: youth and identity in a postcolonial world London and New York: Routledge

Jennings, R and Gardner, A (2012) *'Rock On': Women Ageing and Popular Music* Farnham and Burlington: Ashgate

Kemp, Sandra and Squires, Judith (1997) *Feminisms* Oxford and New York: Oxford University Press

Laing, Dave (1985) *One Chord Wonders: power and meaning in punk rock* Milton Keynes: Open University Press

Leuonard, Marian (2007) *Gender in the Music Industry* Farnham and Burlington: Ashgate

MacKinnon, Catharine A. (2000) "Points against Postmodernism," *Chicago-Kent Law Review*: Vol. 75: Issue.3,Article5.
Available at: http://scholarship.kentlaw.iit.edu/cklawreview/vol75/iss3/5 accessed 19/01/14

McKay, George (1996) *Senseless Acts of Beauty* London and New York: Verso

McRobbie, Angela (1990) 'Settling Accounts with Subcultures: A Feminist Critique' in Frith, Simon and Goodwin, Andrew (eds) (1998) *On Record: rock, pop and the written word* London and New York: Routledge

Moore, Allan (2002) 'Authenticity as Authentication' in *Popular Music*, Vol 21, No 2 (May 2002) pp 209-223, Cambridge: Cambridge University Press

Muggleton, David and Weinzierl, Rupert (2003) *The Post-subcultures Reader* Oxford and New York: Berg

Nehring, Neil (1997) *Popular Music, Gender and Postmodernism: Anger is an Energy.* New York: Sage

Nicholas, Lucy (2007) *Approaches to gender, power and authority in contemporary anarcho-punk: poststructuralist anarchism?* eSharp Issue 9 (Spring 2007) Glasgow:
http://www.gla.ac.uk/departments/esharp/ accessed 31/1/14

Monem, Nadine (ed) (2007) *Riot Grrrl: revolution girl style now!* London:Black Dog Publishing

Phillips, Merle and Brown, Margaret (2012) *It's Different for Girls* [private publication]
Plant. Sadie (1992) *The Most Radical gesture: the Situationist International in the Postmodern Age*. London: Routledge

Potter, Sally, (1997) 'On Shows', in Parker, Roszika, and Pollock, Griselda (eds) (1997) *Framing Feminism: Art and the Womens' Movement 1970-1985* London: Pandora p 30

Radstone, Susannah (1997) 'Postcards from the Edge: Thoughts on the 'Feminist Theory: An international Debate' Conference held at Glasgow University, Scotland, 12-15 July 1991' in Kemp, Sandra and Squires, Judith (1997) *Feminisms* Oxford and New York: Oxford University Press pp104-108

Raha, Maria (2005) *Cinderella's Big Score: women of the punk and indie underground* Emeryville: Seal Press

Reddington, Helen (2012) *The Lost Women of Rock Music: female musicians of the punk era.* London: Equinox

Rowbotham, Sheila (1973, 1981) *Woman's Consciousness, Man's World* Harmondsworth and New York: Penguin

Sabin, Roger (ed) (1999) *Punk Rock: So What? The Cultural Legacy of Punk* London: Routledge

Sabin, Roger (1999) 'Rethinking Punk and Racism' in Sabin, Roger (ed) (1999) *Punk Rock: So What? The Cultural Legacy of Punk* London: Routledge, pp 199-218

Savage, John (1991) *England's Dreaming: Sex Pistols and Punk Rock* London: Faber and Faber

Sontag, Susan (1982) 'Notes on Camp' in *The Susan Sontag Reader* London and New York: Penguin pp105-119

Steward, Sue, and Garratt, Sheryl (1984) *Signed, Sealed and delivered: true life stories of women in pop* London and Sydney: Pluto Press

Walkerdine, Valerie. 1997. *Daddy's Girl: Young Girls and Popular Culture.* Basingstoke and London: Macmillan.

Whiteley, Sheila.(2000) *Women and Popular Music: sexuality, identity and subjectivity* London and New York: Routledge

York, Peter (1980) *Style Wars* London: Sidgwick and Jackson

Young, Rob (2010) *Electric Eden: unearthing Britain's visionary music* London: Faber and Faber

Websites

http://www.poisongirls.co.uk/ **accessed 24/01/14**

www.anarcho-punk.net

http://www.punkbrighton.co.uk

http://womensliberationmusicarchive.co.uk/

http://www.crimethinc.com/

Audio

Crass, *Penis Envy,* 1981, are-release vailable on Crass, 2010

Poison Girls, *Take the Toys*, 1984, available from *Their Finest Moments* 1998, Reactive Records

Film

She's a Punk Rocker UK, Zillah Ashworth, available from www.voiceprint.co.uk

Interviews etc

Author's interviews with Zillah Ashworth, 2003 and 2013

Personal communication with Vi Subversa, 2001

Original Artwork by Persons Unknown used in You're Already Dead by CRASS

IT WAS WHAT IT WAS... "Es delito ser Punk"

... We went searching in the garbage, there was one day a week when, at the Santa Fe[54] garbage dumpsters, hamburgers were dumped and we would go and eat hamburgers from the garbage, in groups we would occupy some abandoned houses and of course it was chaotic because well... we didn't have any rules to follow, I remember that sometimes there was this idea, like one time we were in an abandoned house squat and someone got there with a green liver that he had picked from the garbage, "ok, we'll cook it with lots of onions", everybody stood up and I said "you fools, you'll be getting the bloody typhoid" but no, I don't know if it was because they were sniffing glue or what but they didn't even got diarrhea [...] and then, someone else killed cats to feed the ones who had nothing to eat and we would make a broth and... but because a lot of the people who would get there were inhaling and doing drugs, we couldn't segregate them right?, those were some of the good things, but also they served to sink us you see?

... because among us there were people who were "Panchitos"[55] for example, gang members whose parents had been thugs and thieves and for them it was normal, I mean, for them to say "I smoked a joint, or I've just robbed a guy, I pulled him out some quid" it was normal to hear it at home.

... the police didn't ask, the police would grab, beat and imprison you and... I'll tell you an anecdote too, once we were grabbed by the police, my girlfriend and I, she was raped and I was beaten to a pulp and we were dumped at... the border of Xochiaca[56], the river channel of Xochiaca, they thought we were dead, can you imagine the kind of beat we were given? And we hadn't committed any crime, just the fact that we were different, we looked different. And those are the things that the new generations haven't lived, they don't know, however they indeed want to feel themselves the different kind, the heroes...

We taught the street kids some workshops, I taught "Initiation in the Arts", like art creation. It wasn't really about the workshops themselves, but more like telling them "there are options, other alternatives", but we were faced with really gruesome things: children who have lived in the sewers all their lives and for them it was normal. It happened to me once, while giving a workshop a kid died in the gutter, and... "lets call... lets call the public prosecutor's office and I was told "no man, in here no prosecutor. The kid died and there he stays", and I had to watch him being eaten by the rats, all of it disintegrated and carried away by the sewage.

---

[54] Santa Fe. Although nowadays this region is considered the little Manhattan due to its urban development that started back in the 1990s, Santa Fe was one of the biggest dumpsters of México City for decades.

[55] Panchitos. One of the oldest and probably the most famous gang from México City, back in the 1980s they got so out of control that the government tried very hard to socially re-integrate them in order to get a hold of them, however it was time and not a particular social program which actually took a toll on this gang.

[56] Xochiaca. Inserted in the neighbourhood of Nezahualcoyotl, one of the ever growing dorm cities in the outskirts of México City, el Bordo de Xochiaca is one of the most famous and biggest dumpsters where on top of all the garbage produced by the city, has served as unknown graveyard for the unlucky ones.

[non adapted people] there were a lot, in my generation... let me tell you, there were delinquents, suddenly you were organizing yourself with some others to put up an exhibition at the Chopo Museum[57], and then someone would arrive in haste and would ask "hey, have you seen the cops passing by?" "no, why?" "it's just that I just killed a guy" and what were we supposed to do? I mean, we were not going to denounce him, we couldn't segregate him, in the end as I have told you, it was their conscience and their problems right? Me for example, I carried on the idea for a long time of "if you are a punk, kill a policeman" because I had been brutalized so many times; and then it turned up that sometimes I was told by some other lads "I am a Punk mate" "what are you doing ass?" so I said... I mean, ... and the girl who had been my girlfriend, she kept that idea, she was really hurt, she was... well I think up to date, she still carries on that idea of killing policemen, because as I've told you we had been assaulted and dumped.

A STORY... OF SO FEW... "San Felipe es Punk"

Well I am from the San Felipe[58] neighbourhood, there it was supposed that Punk in Mexico originated, why? Well from there was Javier Beviera[59] [sic] who was one of the initiators, he was in a band called Decibel[60] back then, and then from Decibel, Walter Schmidt created Size[61] and Javier Baviera

---

[57] Chopo Museum. Museo Universitario del Chopo – Acquired in 1903 at the Great Industrial Exhibition in Dusseldorf, Germany, dismounted and brought to México City to become proof of progress and mondernity within the 100 years celebration of the Independence of México in 1910, the Museum has gone through a long and hectic History; belonging since 1971 to the National Autonomous University in México, it is on the 4th of October 1980 that the Institution, the sacred Museum opens its doors to the first and so far only Rock trading space in those days where independen record labels, collectors, musicians and people in general could attend to trade their records, know more about the music they were enjoying and support the independent rock scene. A forum that surpassed the limits of the device.

[58] Colonia San Felipe de Jesus. In the farthest part of the Gustavo A. Madero county, in the northwest side of México Citiy, the Neighbourhood San Felipe de Jesus claims itself a bastion of the Punk Movement in México, by sheltering the self-proclaimed first Punk band "Rebel´d´Punk", Javier Baviera, its founder, not originally from San Felipe de Jesús, moved there as a teenager and found akin spirits to give birth to what later would be recognized as Mexican Punk Music.

[59] Javier Baviera. Originally from the neighbourhood of Tepito, better know as one of the oldest street-markets and for their tight ties to their turf and among their inhabitants, Javier Baviera, first a saxophonist of the Experimental Band "Decibel", when he moves to the neighbourhood of San Felipe de Jesús, and influenced by the Punk movement that was re-sounding in the United States via Tijuana and Illy Bleeding, singer of Size and Dangerous Rhythm, founds the band Rebel´D´Punk, arguably the first Punk band in the country.

[60] Decibel. Known as Rock in Opposition, Decibel is, in lack of a better description, an experimental band from the 1970s whose influences go from progressive, jazz, avant-garde rock, free improvisation and so forth. Founded by Walter Schmidt the band has had several guest musicians along its few and cult considered recordings. One of those guest musicians was Javier Baviera.

[61] Size. As a side project from Decibel, Walter Schmidt meets Jaime Keller, a.k.a. Illy Bleeding, a bourgeois touched and influenced during his time living in New York by the Punk Movement and the New Wave musicians, giving birth to Size, a more inclined Post-Punk band that nonetheless is put to compete against Rebel´D´Punk as to which band is the first Mexican Punk Band, however, the difference in class, sometimes gives Rebel´D´Punk the preference among the audience. It is important to remark that neither Illy Bleeding nor Javier Baviera ever kept strife or anything of the sort, on the contrary, they both, in their time helped each other as much.

created Rebel'd'Punk[62], then at the Secondary School that I attended, because I always say that I breastfed Punk from there, I met people like Aknez[63], the Zappa[64], the Boa and many more with whom later on discovered the movement.

From 79 till 82, more accurately during the 1980 because when we got into Secondary School I was already a rocker, I was a fan of Kiss, and for example, with me there was Dan Caries[65] who is the singer for Rebel'd'Punk right now, and is the brother of Arturo who also founded Rebel with Javier Baviera, so imagine, there we came together and we started the movement. Actually my band there suddenly we were all punks!! Once a prefect came and said "we're here to confiscate everything that is not part of the uniform" and she took like 3 humongous bags, full with buttons and the buttons were really hard to get back then, of neckerchiefs and the uniform pants we painted them like chess boards and... and.. well.. and it was something like punk but it wasn't like "I'm just trying to get your attention" but it was more like "someone took it from somewhere" and we adopted it so I think that, that was part of the Secondary School No. 185 where a lot of us adopted punk because we were living it.

So there it was born, you start meeting people, then you come to the Chopo[66], you bump into more lads and then you start getting to know the lads. And it was during that time when we started to work with the concept of punk, it belonged at the beginning to the Gangs, there were the PND[67], the lads from "El Molinito" and so on.

I was from the San Felipe neighbourhood, but I didn't belong to any gang... look, in that sense I was never a delinquent, because my first experience as a delinquent, I can tell you that it was when I was 13 years old, I picked up a brick and threw it away breaking a window from a house... and I just heard

---

[62] Rebel'd'Punk. Founded in the heart of the lads neigbourhood, "Tepito", Rebel´D´Punk, one of the first Punk Bands in México found its niche and crib in the neighbourhood of "San Felipe de Jesús", founded by Javier Baviera it has kept itself alive with different musicians for more than 20 years now with epic songs such as "De Plástico" (of Plastic), "Museo del Chopo" and "Es delito ser Punk" (It's a crime to be Punk)

[63] Aknez. Singer of the now disappeared band "Masacre 68" famous for its anarchic and often questioning lyrics such as "No estamos conformes" (We do not agree)

[64] Zappa Punk. Singer, Zinester and Activist, Patricia Moreno Rodríguez a.k.a. Zappa Punk was the singer of "Virgninidad Sacudida" the first all-grrrls punk band back in the 1980s. She was also part of CHAPS (Colectivo de las Chavas Activas Punk) and Colectivo Cambio Radical Fuerza Positiva, the first one originally an all girls Collective. Later on she became the singer of SS-20 "Secta Suicida Siglo XX" a punk band that intended to encapsulate the urban neurosis of the 1980s that disbanded in 1991.

[65] Dan Caries. Daniel Beristain is the brother of Arturo Beristain alias "El Soldado", both along with Javier Baviera founded Rebel´D´Punk and later one, when Javier left the band to live in the United States of America, Arturo and Dan re-formed Rebel´D´Punk giving it new life for more than 20 years.

[66] Chopo. El Tianguis Cultural del Chopo. The Cultural Street Market – Borned within the walls of the device/institution the Chopo Museum, the originally trading space kept the name of his "daddy", known as "El Chopo", has been for more than 30 years THE Rock Street Market in the whole country. Known internationally, the son of the system became bigger in its rupture with it and keeps on rocking every saturday as the space to be and let be.

[67] PND. Standing for Punk not Dead was one of the first Punk Collectives during the 1980s that became the Cambio Radical Fuerza Positiva, releasing itself from the violent generation shaped by gangs such as Los Panchitos.

screaming of so many people and I got the sensation that I had beaten someone that didn't even deserve it... so I said "well... gangs no" and also that same day at night, I got to look a guy whose head was smashed with one of those metal gutter plates. So I don't know if I got scared or... or... really I said "violence... is not for me" but I used to talk with a lot of gangs, [...] the problems among gangs and their deeds have harmed us as social group because suddenly some of us were very conscious people who were really working, and our work would be obscured by the smallest gang deed as opposed to the great work we had been doing. And up to date is still like that, a lot of places were lost, but fortunately there have always been conscious people that really work, but there have also been people that... well, they are just here (in the movement) because of the party time, that follow only the media which states that " if you are punk, you are a drug-addict, a thug and... violent" and finally I mean, currently the movement is less... mmm how shall I say it?... mmm dogmatized, because in the past for example I was punk and I used to listen to reggae and the others would look at me like "are you Caribbean or what" I mean... and today no, now you can listen to pretty much everything.

IT´S ALL ABOUT THE MUSIC... "Anarquía"

Of Punk the first band I heard were The Ramones and the Sex Pistols, and from the underground I got an Italian compilation, that included a band called Eyescream[68] and... and I liked them a lot, I mean, it contained two songs from them and they were my favourites and... Plastic Bertrand, a French that actually... he sings that song "trans en pom are pom are" [sic] (Ca Plane Pour Moi) which is the famous one, actually it was... mmm... everything you could get your hands on, because we would listen to bands like the B52, that now you don't consider them as punks, and... but the most commercial music we got were The Six Pistols and The Ramones, from the underground that Italian compilation, and I loved it, there was this one song called "No a la policia" and it started with a scream "there comes the police" in Italian right? [...] and it's just that in the past it was really hard to get anything punk, it was like... how can I explain?, a button, a button... you ended up making it because they were only sold at Hip 70[69], really bloody expensive and of Punk you wouldn't find much, you would find for sure the one from the Sex Pistols. I still have it, all broken but it's a relic, stored and well... those were the first bands I listened to. In Spanish... I think they were Eskorbuto and La Polla,[70] and of course, Código Neurótico[71] were the ones that got to me musically because I've always said that Punk wasn't a musical movement in essence but a social one, because if you take a look at the very first bands, from them you got the Dark movement, the Thrash movement, the New Wave, the New Rock and it was more like an attitude right? "I'm going against the system because I disagree with it" and based upon that a lot of good things came

---

[68] From Punk Rock World web site, Group information on Eyescream: http://www.punkrockworld.it/web.testing/?sezione=gruppo&pagina=show&ordine=grNome&azione=show&id=0&gruppo=Eyescream&lingua=eng

[69] Hip 70. Originally a Record Store of Imported Albums, albums that were next to impossible to find anywhere else back in the 1960s, with time it turned out to be an underground club where experimental bands used to play, such is the case of Size who later became for some, the 1st punk band that mostly was into the Post-Punk movement.

[70] Eskorbuto and La Polla Records. Basque and Spanish Mythical Punk Bands.

[71] Código Neurótico. Spanish Punk Band

out and a lot of bad ones too right? So it was... my generation for example, we got to experiment a lot right? And there were good and not that good results.

COMITTMENT, PARTY, NOISE... "Fiesta"

Look, I think that indeed there was a bit the disorderly noisy freedom because we were told about Punk and Anarchism, Anarchism equals disorder, according to the dictionary, but within that there was a certain awareness because [...] we would get together and if we were in disagreement with something we would organize together a demonstration right? Actually mmm... lots of the very first actions carried out were to show society that we weren't bad people, the first expositions of the Caos Urbano[72], which was one of the first ones carried out by the Punks, was to state why we dressed as we did right? Because on those days the attire really had a specific meaning, for example if you were dressed in black it was because you really thought there was no future and you were mourning yourself, if you ripped your clothes and all, it was because you were against the system, it meant "I don't want to be all tailored and pretty when in reality this society is giving us shit", actually my generation was very much into going to the dumpsters and through the garbage, tearing clothes a little bit more, painting them and that was our attire right? [...] lots of torn clothes mostly, today is not like that, today there are a lot of patches, so now I see this kids with expensive trousers but with patches. And we weren't like that, we... I... I as a plastic and visual artist, work with recycled material but I mean, I always used it, I've always worn clothes from the trash, always... I've got to wear even the bottle-top caps so I would look, in a way, different. So one of the firsts mottos was to break up with the establishment, and breaking up with the establishment meant exactly that "I'll do what you don't like."

DO IT YOURSELF... "Chamarras Negras"

Well, actually at the beginning we didn't work with the D.I.Y. ethos, I think the D.I.Y. idea got to us like... in the middle or late 1985 when we started thinking a little bit more in organizing ourselves. Because for example, when it comes to Collectives, the first one to emerge as Collective, not as Gang, was "Cambio Radical"[73] because we got news that there was a Collective in Italy called "Virus Collective" and, in a certain way, we told to ourselves, let see who wants in right? [...] ... when a Collective is organized, you start thinking of something else, what is a Collective? What are you going to do with that Collective? And then we started thinking about making a fanzine, exhibitions, organizing... actually the ones who started to work with Anarchism, the Anarchy from the United Kingdom, were the Six Pistols, cause as I told you, the idea here was what was stated in the Thesaurus as "Anarchy equals Disorder" however, it was the prod for you to start researching for real what was Anarchism and then got you interested really on what was Anarchy and if... now, one of the mistakes committed by the new generations is that "I am an Anarchist and super dogmatic" right? And I say, "chill out mate, you're just

---

[72] Caos Urbano 2. Was an exhibition / gig / workshop / conference all together not only to create a space for Punks in the middle of the 1980s to be free to express themselves but for the interested and not so interested members of a discriminative society to know, understand and learn about a subculture that was mostly linked, due to a vicious press, to violence, vandalism and crime.

[73] Cambio Radical. The Collective Cambio Radical Fuerza Positiva, originally from the Punk Not Dead collective was the head behind the exhibition Caos Urbano 2 and many more events and actions influenced by the Anarchy ideas from Bakunin and the Flores Magón brothers.

missing your potato and there you go right?" because if... I say, dogmatism is the greatest expression of stupidity, and you can have it in many ways: religious dogmatism, moral dogmatism even artistic dogmatism right? You can say "I do this and because you are not with me..."; but in the end all that are power cues, "I can do this and I won't share it with you, I've got power, more than you." So you can see how that is one of the greatest mistakes right now.

FANZINES... GOING FURTHER... "No estamos conformes"

Well, the thing is that before doing my own Fanzine, I worked for a lot of fanzines. We started doing as I told you before, the one for "Cambio Radical" [...] so when I decided to create my own fanzine was because I wanted to express myself [...] and with a Bachelor in Arts, I wanted to say things.

And how did you take the decision of studying a Bachelor in Arts? The reason I ask is because, in a way, I've felt or seen that many of the people involved in the Punk movement, have always excused themselves by stating that they didn't have the opportunity to study or do something else.

For me those are excuses and I'll tell you why. One time in a meeting we had at the Chopo, someone was saying, "well I don't have a job"... because I stated before: "you should stop asking money from people right? That gives us a bad image" and someone responded "the reason I ask for money to people on the street is because I don't get a job and I don't know... I don't want to be nobody's slave, I don't want to be exploited", "very well then, buy yourself a box of bubble-gum and nobody will exploit you, you will sell the gum when you want, you'll earn the money you want with it and when you want to do it; if you just want to sustain your basic needs or if you want to become millionaire you'll be able to do it, but it is your decision." Sometimes we nail ourselves to the given frameworks to excuse ourselves and say: "well, it cannot be done" we state: "it's just that I don't do this, I don't that because I got segregated" and I'm telling you, personally I segregated myself for a long time until I realized the power I had within the culture that I was creating, what I was writing actually had a certain liking for the rest of the people, sometimes we justify our idleness, our mistakes by blaming the system. "It's just that they won't accept me" but sometimes it is us the ones who haven't accepted ourselves, we haven't discovered the real value that we have and we stop looking for our own alternatives, which does not mean that you have to do something that the rest should like. [...] ... there are people that... follow a lot of... people from within our group that I can tell you, have stolen a lot by exploiting the rest of the lads; still, on that matter my conscience is clear. In the end, if I have struggled all my life in order to break with the establishment, to improve the system and if I follow the same pattern as they then I am scum, however you want to see it. And even if I have to suffer hunger, if I only got a little to eat, just to keep myself true to what I am doing, I'll do it, I believe in what I do; I mean, that's the difference when you really believe and when you don't.

I was telling you that Punk got me to medicine because we, as a Collective, organized ourselves when our anarchic tie was to aid social needs, when we realized that we were living in a country where there is hunger then we organized ourselves as a group and created the Collective... "Cocina A."[74] It was... the A was for Alternative Cooking or Kitchen, Anarchic... I still have some logos that I did where

---

[74] Cocina A. Kitchen A

there is a punk with a Wheat Mohawk. The Collective was about experimenting, because, I had more time within the movement but there were newcomers, couples mostly that were trying to have a life together and they used to say "Ok... I'm pregnant and I want to better feed my child"; so it was useful for us, the experimentation because we were cooking in search of our economy, in search of a good nutrition and we started the workshops, we went to where people asked us to go saying that they wanted to learn how to cook with soy and we said "ok". And it was a really really amazing Collective because it did a lot... like a gig for the "Ruta 100"[75] strike, and... also to have fun. We gave out food, here at the Chopo Street Market we gave food three times, to homeless kids, we fed them too, several times. So it was really good because it was another way of organizing as a rocker but thinking more about family integration.

... We would go to the Central de Abastos[76] to ask for the food that was about to go bad. Actually mmm... here at the Chopo street-market something quite curious happened to us because... we did a... a humungous pot of Picadillo[77], it turned out that because we didn't have a fridge, when we got here the food was rotten already, the tomato went bad. A mate told me "hey this is completely bad" and suddenly a thought "well... like fine restaurants mate, we wash it", so we placed it under water to get rid of all the tomato and the sauce, "ok... go get some jars of mayonnaise" and we mixed the meat with it and we called it... Russian Picadillo and it was really successful, you have no idea because we were giving the tacos for free to those that we knew didn't have money and the bus drivers we would sell the tacos and there were some that got 10 tacos!!!

EXPERIMENTING... REINVENTING

The less. Yes, because unfortunately look... it was what we were discussing before, not everybody could dye his/her hair. For us, dying our hair... first we were poor teenagers, so we were told that with onion we could have our hair dyed and we tried it, indeed in helps to bleach but it wasn't too good, then with hydrogen peroxide water... and then the colour, back in those days there were no brands so it was our own invention those little drops[78]. That was our invention cause I'll tell you, at the beginning we would use water-based paint, markers, you would grab the marker and once you'd got your Mohawk up you would paint it with the marker, or some acrylic paint, the kind you use to paint the walls. At the gigs, once they were finished we were all covered in paint because it had drained and mixed with the sweat. [...] Back in those days we would use vegetable ink, the one used to paint tamales. We bought the little packet, it was around 1 peso, dissolved it and used it. [To get our Mohawks, we used natural gelatine] ...

---

[75] Ruta 100. Red de Transporte de Pasajeros, was the name of one of the Public Transportation Systems in México City, which dealt with Buses and Trolley Buses. Because it was subsidized by the Government, it was very cheap; working from 1981 till 1995 when it went broke due to pressures to have it privatized, in 1989 it went on strike demanding better payments, the strike was the beginning of the end.

[76] Central de Abastos. Central Groceries Center. Is the main Wholesale market of foods and groceries in México City. Built to be the mainpoint for producers, wholesalers, retailers and consumers of the entire country, it is located in the eastern county of Iztapalapa.

[77] Picadillo. Minced meat in tomato sauce

[78] Gotas de color. Coloured Drops, back in the 1980s and 1990s, the best way to dye hair in psychedelic colours was the drops, made with vegetable ink, water and something else... the color would run away after 2 or 3 washes but for the immediate purpose of coloring it was better than markers.

and to dry it we would all blow air at each other... it wasn't like "hey... I've got a dryer let's do it" no... I mean it was... eh... eh... it was all about experimentation and that was the fun part too.

WHO... WHEN... HOW... AND THEN? "Divisiones Absurdas"

Well, it's just that there were different stages. We can talk about a first generation, the strong part was from the ending of the 1980s but then there was a whole displacement of those people who suddenly had some other stuff to do and new people took their place, [...] it happened to me, suddenly after finishing my bachelor I had to work, and people that I knew who didn't know anything suddenly became leaders with different ideas. So there have been different stages, some might have been good, some might have been productive, the mistake has been not analysing the History, I mean "because now I am the protagonist, I don't give a damn, you may think yourself a super hero but now you are old and terminated, so you are no longer useful" and they don't realize that sometimes, knowing what the other one did and the bumps in the road he faced, could be very useful to not fall again. Not to keep the same line because in the end, what served us was the experimentation, with its positive and negative results.

I said "ok, in the end I keep my own way" I did everything I wanted, I mean, I can really tell you that to me, the Punk movement really provided me with an alternative of life, because if I hadn't been punk, I think I would have never exploited all these... artistry and creativity... the Punk was really motivational for me in order to do a lot of stuff, to break up with the schemes that had been imposed in my house.

FOREVER YOUNG OR FOREVER PUNK...?

Well... I study Acupuncture. Actually as I've told you... the Punk movement led me to the Alternative Medicine.

No look, I believe that within the experimentation, you got yourself into a lot of things. There were stages when we were alcoholics, or very... eh... sexually active and exhibitionists. We got together to drink and we ended up naked, so everything got its place.

The experimentation emerged in the Cooking Collective, we started with the nutritional stuff, we became vegetarians, and some people said "this is so good, I like those weird punks that are thinking about eating properly, I'll give them a medicine workshop" and I got connected with a certain group, I got in, I learned how to give massages, I learned uhm... several stuff that little by little led me, and finally the vision I've got of medicine is to help people.

Within the Cooking Collective, the concept under which I worked was: I'll teach people how to make their own soymilk and at the same time I'll tell them how the government is exploiting them. That they don't have enough money because the great industries are absorbing everything, so how am I rebelling with them? By creating my own cooking alternative, then I started following the path to Health, of taking that syrup, rubbing that unguent... the acupuncture... my linkages I always say have been Art, Medicine and uhm... and Punk.

I mean, I am someone... here they are always mocking me because I always wear different stuff and I actually studied fashion design in order to make myself my own clothes first, and second I am always roaming the different street-markets trying to check the different stuff [...] to me it was easier and up to date and I paint my own t-shirts with acrylics, stating my own messages because that makes me more... mmm... particular, more me, I am wearing this and nobody else is wearing what I am.

The fact that I do these things is because first, I can and second because I want things to be this way. To me, the Punk movement indeed was an alternative, you can do this and you neither need nor have to tie yourself to the system or anybody, and I won't become stupid and state "bloody system" I believe that sometimes we blame the system to avoid our own responsibility. Everything in life has to be worked for, if you are interested in doing something, put some effort to it, but there are a lot of people who want the easy way through tings. But I'll be a creator, not a copy.

Oral History of Marcos Suárez, "El Marilyn", alternative medicine practitioner, visual and fashion artist but above all Punk to his backbone in México.

Rob Miller – Amebix – by Jacky Smith

Disgustin' Justin *Justine Butler*

The 1970's was the decade of power cuts, the three-day-week and public sector strikes. In 1976 these was a massive heat wave, I remember a hosepipe ban and people sneaking out to water their gardens at night. Then in 1978 came the winter of discontent. Ambulance drivers, firemen and nurses went on strike. Gravediggers downed tools and bodies piled up. The bin men stopped collecting and rubbish was piled high in the streets attracting rats in London. The headlines ripped the Labour government to shreds and paved the way for Thatcher's electoral victory in 1979. The cold war loomed large and I thought we were all going to die in a nuclear war. The horror of the thermonuclear flash filled my dreams. There was a sense of impending doom and I felt like I had nothing to lose. Then I discovered punk. It was like an injection of adrenalin! Suddenly there was something to shout about, the new music was full of energy and anger. I wanted to make the most of it, to be part of it, it fitted like a glove.

Things we regard as superficial now carried a huge importance in the 70's. If you dyed your hair red, blue or green, heads would turn, people would shout at you in the street and only men who'd done time in the navy or prison had tattoos. I cut my long mousy brown hair short, spiked it up, died it blue and discarded the desert boots and blanket coat for DMs and an old man's raincoat I'd found at a jumble sale. I thought I was the bee's knees! I recently heard Lebanese poet Kahlil Gibran's description of how he felt wearing his new suit; it made him stand out and feel good, it was magical. His description transported me back to being a teenage punk.

On my 16th birthday, a boy I didn't know very well arrived at my Mum's house with a pair of new DMs for me, (I'd only had my boyfriend's cast offs until then). He also bought me a brand new pair of black bondage trousers, they were amazing. Every time I put them on I felt like I was walking on air... I was invincible! I wrote the names of the bands I liked on my old granddad shirt: Devo, Sex Pistols, Stranglers, Clash.... I noticed nods of approval from the two punk boys in the year above me at school, who were both called Alan! Funny how all the same rules applied. Wearing a uniform, seeking approval, wanting credibility... we weren't so radical but it felt like a new freedom. I listened to everything I could get my hands on 999, X-Ray Spex, The Ramones, The Damned, Siouxsie and the Banshees, The Ruts, Wayne/Jayne County, Buzzcocks, the Vibrators... I spent all my pocket on records. I had songs for different things, if I was angry I'd play *Sometimes* by the Stranglers. My getting ready to go out songs were *You're Ready Now* by Slaughter and the Dogs or something by Siouxsie – *Metal Postcard* was a favourite. I once dumped a boyfriend by playing the Angelic Upstart's *Leave Me Alone*. I am sure I can still smell glue every time I hear The Ruts *West One (Shine on Me)*.

Over the next year or two I discovered anarcho-punk; Flux of Pink Indians, Rudimentary Peni, Poison Girls and of course, Crass. I soaked up the lyrics. Everything we had been told about family, relationships, society and work was shit. It was all a bunch of lies, designed to fool us and make us submit. I was no fool, society owed me a living! That didn't go down too well with my hard-working Mum who was a single parent and a school teacher... she was amazingly tolerant given what a twat I was. One day, I got called in to see the headmaster at my school and he said there had been complaints about my blue hair and he was worried it might jeopardise the school's future by influencing peoples' decision where to send their kids! The Council were threatening to axe one of the schools in Welwyn Garden City at the time and he suggested my blue hair might be a contributing factor to an unfavourable decision. Even at my young age I knew that was ludicrous! He asked what my parents thought of my blue hair and I said my Dad didn't live with us and my Mum had died it blue for me. She also made countless miniskirts and my favourite trousers ever - black and white leopard print fluffy drainpipes! She made them out of an old coat I had picked up at Portobello market. She encouraged self-expression and gave me a sense of self confidence that would help me survive some quite hairy situations that were soon to come…

The best bit about growing up near London was I got to go to loads of gigs at the Rainbow, the Lyceum, Hammersmith Palais and Hammersmith Odeon. Smaller venues and pubs like the 100 Club, Dingwalls, the Fulham Greyhound and the George Robey put on smaller bands and several people I knew played in those venues. I loved the little local gigs too like Rudimentary Peni at the Ludwig Youth Club in Welwyn Garden City and Crass at Bowes Lyon in Stevenage.

Gigs could be very violent. In September 1980, when I heard Crass were playing down the road in Stevenage I was ecstatic! It was one train stop away and I was definitely going. None of the boys I knew would come with me, they were too scared. They said it was going to be a massive punch up but I wasn't going to be put off. To be fair, I think it was worse for boys. I got on the train on my own and went along full of excitement and anticipation. At the venue, I pushed my way down to the front and as soon as Crass started playing all these big skinheads appeared and started punching all the young punks. They were twice the size of us! I clambered onto the stage and cowered under the bassist Pete Wright. A young lad (he couldn't have been much older than 14 or 15) lunged at the monitor and was gripping on with all his strength, the skinheads had hold of him and one was hammering on his head with his fist while they tried to pull him back into the crowd, I could see his fingers slipping. I reached out and grabbed his arm and I think some others helped, somehow we managed to get him on the stage and he joined me under the bassist who carried on playing until the singer, Steve Ignorant, couldn't take the Nazi salutes and shouts of 'sieg heil' anymore and launched himself off the stage into the middle of it all. I think that might have been the end of the gig. It's all a bit blurred. There was another fight at the train station and a bloke I knew had to decide between getting beaten up by skinheads or running over the tracks into the arms of the British Transport Police, he went for the cops and got nicked. Interestingly the worse gig for violence I ever went to wasn't a punk gig, it was The Specials, Madness and The Selector at Hatfield Polytechnic in 1979, the skinheads had Stanley knives at that one.

I fucked up my A' levels. O' levels had been a doss and I thought I could just breeze through again but my results were not good. I got an O grade in sociology and an F for history and art. My results spelt OFF! So I got a job working at the dirty end of an industrial dishwasher in a local school for a year while I retook sociology. I needed an A' level for a grant for college. I retook the exam and managed to scrape through with an E and moved to St Albans where I attended the art college, briefly.

St Albans was a violent place in those days and a friend's younger brother had been murdered just before I got there. Apparently he had been wearing a drape jacket and his punky spikey hair had pissed someone off to the extent that they had stabbed him and killed him… I didn't go into college much, in fact after three months I went in and said I thought I should leave. They agreed and said they were about to boot me out anyway…

I moved into a squat, an old dentists' building and just pissed about until one night I was followed home and attacked. I was wearing my customary miniskirt, spikey-heeled boots, Siouxsie make up and probably had a bit of a swagger on. This guy followed me down the road screaming what a slag I looked like and calling me every name you can think of (for a woman). He eventually caught me up and punched me in the face, both feet left the ground. I had broken teeth, a fractured cheekbone and a punctured sinus… When I look back at that incident I think it was a surprise to both of us, but I do hope it was the last time that he hit a woman, or anyone for that matter! They asked me some outrageous questions in court. I was asked if my boyfriend was going to be spending the night with me that night and how often he stayed over. They asked if I hated men. If I was a feminist and if I'd ever spat at anyone. They wanted to see how high my heels were. My Mum's friend jumped to his feet and shouted at one point and was threatened with being evicted from the court. Finally it was over, the bloke who hit me got a record for GBH and I left town. He never knew that I turned down three offers to have the matter settled let's say privately.

I had been intending on moving to London but I'd met a couple on a demo in London who lived in a squat in Bristol and they said I could come and stay anytime. So I got on a bus to Bristol with a mate. We arrived late but found the place quite easily; it took up the whole corner of a street just up from the centre. The building was due to be knocked down so it was called the Demolition Ballroom, it was an old car showroom used for gigs. The Demolition Diner was a cheap friendly café where you could buy lunch for 50p. Mostly frequented by young punks and squatters, a few professionals would come in, the odd left-wing solicitor with a briefcase or bearded social worker, there was also a bookshop called Full Marks that sold anarchist books and stuff (a friend ran his independent record company out of there too), upstairs there was a meeting room and a few bedrooms.

Everyone was very friendly and welcoming although our immediate trip to the off licence over the road was met with disapproval from one of the older anarchists. I remember him sitting around drinking coffee banging on about Nicaragua and peering over his *Guardian* to ask us when we were moving out. We didn't stay long.

I arrived in the midst of a rift between two groups that nearly got nasty. The feminists were angry about a poster by the anti-fur group Lynx. It featured a model dragging a blood-soaked fur coat with the slogan "it takes up to 40 dumb animals to make a fur coat but only one to wear it". They said they were going to deface the poster as was offensive to women. The animal rights lot said if anyone defaced it, they would deface them! I was a vegan by then and sympathised with the animal rights lot but I was also a feminist and didn't like the macho posturing. They were always coming back from hunt-sabbing covered in mud flexing their muscles going on about what a good ruck it had been. Some of them should have joined the army I thought.

Soon after arriving in Bristol I bought a drum kit and joined an all-girl punk band. I learnt to drum to the 999 song *Homicide*, it's got a very simple beat. Our band was called Rita and the Piss Artists and we weren't very good but we played a few gigs and got a mention in the music journal *Maximum Rocknroll*. I used to have a can or two of Red Stripe before playing and my memory is a bit foggy but I do remember playing at the Demolition Ballroom and a mate who was also a drummer leaning over the front of the stage shouting at me "Can't you drum any faster?" It really was that easy to be in a band, most people I knew were in a band at one time or another, quite a few still are!

Around this time I had my first experience with heroin, not as a user but seeing it used. I was taken round to a house to meet some new people, it was a scruffy old squat, grubby and dark inside. There was a bloke sat in the corner who asked me if I had a light. I took my lighter over to him and saw all the drug paraphernalia... a teaspoon, the wrap, the needle... I was shocked but tried not to show it. It was pretty commonplace in Bristol among the young punks during the 80's. The author Melvin Burgess wrote an excellent novel about it called *Junk*. This would later be on the syllabus for many GCSE and A' level students including my half-sister! My old mate bicycle Richard was one of the main characters. Disgustin' Justin' he used to call me!

It was pre-Aids days; we just weren't that aware of the danger. I remember being in a room with about 12 other people and a needle going round full of speed. It was just me and one other fella that said no thanks, there was blood in the syringe. I'd been hanging round with bikers before I left home. As all bikers know, every now and then, one of them dies. They get knocked off or hit something and fall off and sometimes a big lorry goes over them. That's what happened to my friend Dick when he was 19. Now it was heroin killing people. I'd been to Portugal for a week or two. We had managed to get return flights for just £13, so a gang of us had been over to piss about in the Algarve. It had been fun and had I thrown my return ticket away and spent a week or two hitching back through Portugal. I got home to hear that a friend had been found dead in his flat a day earlier. He knew he was would die young, he had joked about how he would die before he was 21. That was 30 years ago and I know people that still miss him now.

Not long after that another friend with a taste for heroin died but he was murdered. Something to do with a deal that had gone wrong and an argument followed and he was stabbed and died. Again, I am not sure he was ever going to make it as an old man. He had '99% is shit' tattooed on one side of his face and 'goat's breath' written on the other. The first time I met him, he kicked open the door and came stamping into the room wearing a German army helmet and roaring. Probably about one in four didn't make it out of the gang of punks I knew back then. That's a pretty high rate of loss I think...

Not many of the old punks who are still around have a pension, or a retirement plan. I really don't think we thought we would get old, I certainly didn't and I guess most of us were on the dole for a considerable time too. Back then I thought we were all going to go up in smoke. In In 1981 I saw the TV documentary *The War Game*. It was played at a venue in Stevenage called Bowes Lyon, and it was followed by Benjamin Zephaniah then Discharge. Apparently this TV documentary-style drama showing the effects of nuclear war on Britain was deemed too horrifying to broadcast when it was made in 1965 and it wasn't shown in full on TV until 1985. I remember all the young punks sat on the floor looking on in horror at the simulated effects and consequences of a nuclear war in Britain.

A year later in 1982 Raymond Brigg's published his graphic novel *When the Wind Blows*. It shows how an old retired couple, Jim and Hilda Bloggs try to cope with the aftermath of a nuclear attack on Britain by the Soviet Union. Although it was drawn in the style of a comic it was harrowing. The images stuck and I lived in the shadow of this ever-present threat.

One sunny morning in 1984 I woke to hear the air-raid siren blaring. *'This is it'* I thought, in my half-stupor I stumbled through the house and out into the back yard and stood looking up at the sky in my knickers and skimpy t-shirt, waiting for the bomb... it was then my housemate Steve, whose window I was standing directly outside, said "What the fuck are you doing?" then the music started, he was playing the extended 12" version of Frankie Goes to Hollywood's *Two Tribes*, it begins with an air-raid siren. Didn't I feel stupid? That was the second time I'd heard the siren and thought I was about to die. A year or two earlier, sirens had gone off in my home town one particularly windy night. A few of my friends had woken up too and we all thought the same thing – is that it? Then we all just dozed off again...

Living in the shadow of a nuclear war it felt like we had to live for the moment. I was very hedonistic and just wanted to have a laugh most of the time. Planning for the future was never a consideration. This was the consensus among many of the punks I ended up hanging about with. They were the funniest, most ruthless and wittiest people I have ever met. We were all on the dole but most days was someone's giro day, which meant a gallon or two of cider would bought and shared and so most days were like a party! I would often find semi-conscious people on the loo or in the shared sitting room. People would have an eyebrow shaved off, or worse! We were pretty rotten to each other. I once bashed a whole through a partition wall, put my hand through and yanked the record player needle off the Bob Dylan album my housemate was listening to. He wasn't amused. Nor did he find it funny when the power to the top floor of our four-story house failed (that's where his room was). It turned out another housemate had put a bit of masking tape on the fuse for the top floor, he was fed up with the constant electric guitar playing! One particular bloke who thought he was a bit hard earned the nickname 'mashed potato hands' because "he punched like a girl". Then there was the time someone's dead dog was dug up and put on the stairs in an action pose - shocking!

Some of the squats we had were pretty basic. I once mistakenly opened the front door to two men from the local electricity company, they pushed their way in and disabled our supply. So we used candles and street lamps and there was a wood burner in one of the rooms. One day, we had the wood burner blazing for several hours and for some reason I just turned on the hot tap in the kitchen and fuck me - hot water came out! There was a back boiler attached to the wood burner. I ran up the stairs and ran a big hot bath up to my neck, one of my housemates jumped in too. We were so excited about hot water!

The experiences I had were not all good and I wouldn't want my child to share too many of them but they helped me learn some important lessons in life and I was able to use them to become an independent-thinking person who possesses a healthy disrespect for authority and tries to question everything! The friendships I made back then have stood the test of time and when the band The Mob reformed recently after a 30-year hiatus, a huge number of old faces turned up from as far afield as Norway. It was great to see the familiar rogues' gallery of old school punks, degenerates, revellers and rascals. Only now a lot of the women are a bit rounder and the fellas are balding or grey-haired with beer bellies! The warmth (and piss taking) between old friends was heart-warming, at one point we had around the table a traffic warden, a molecular biologist, a school janitor, a film director and a drugs counsellor and the gloves were off like no time had passed. There was of course the next generation of blue-haired miniskirt-wearing studded leather jacket kids to which I am proud to hand the mantle to. I hope they know what to do with it.

Poetry Pieces *Laura Way*

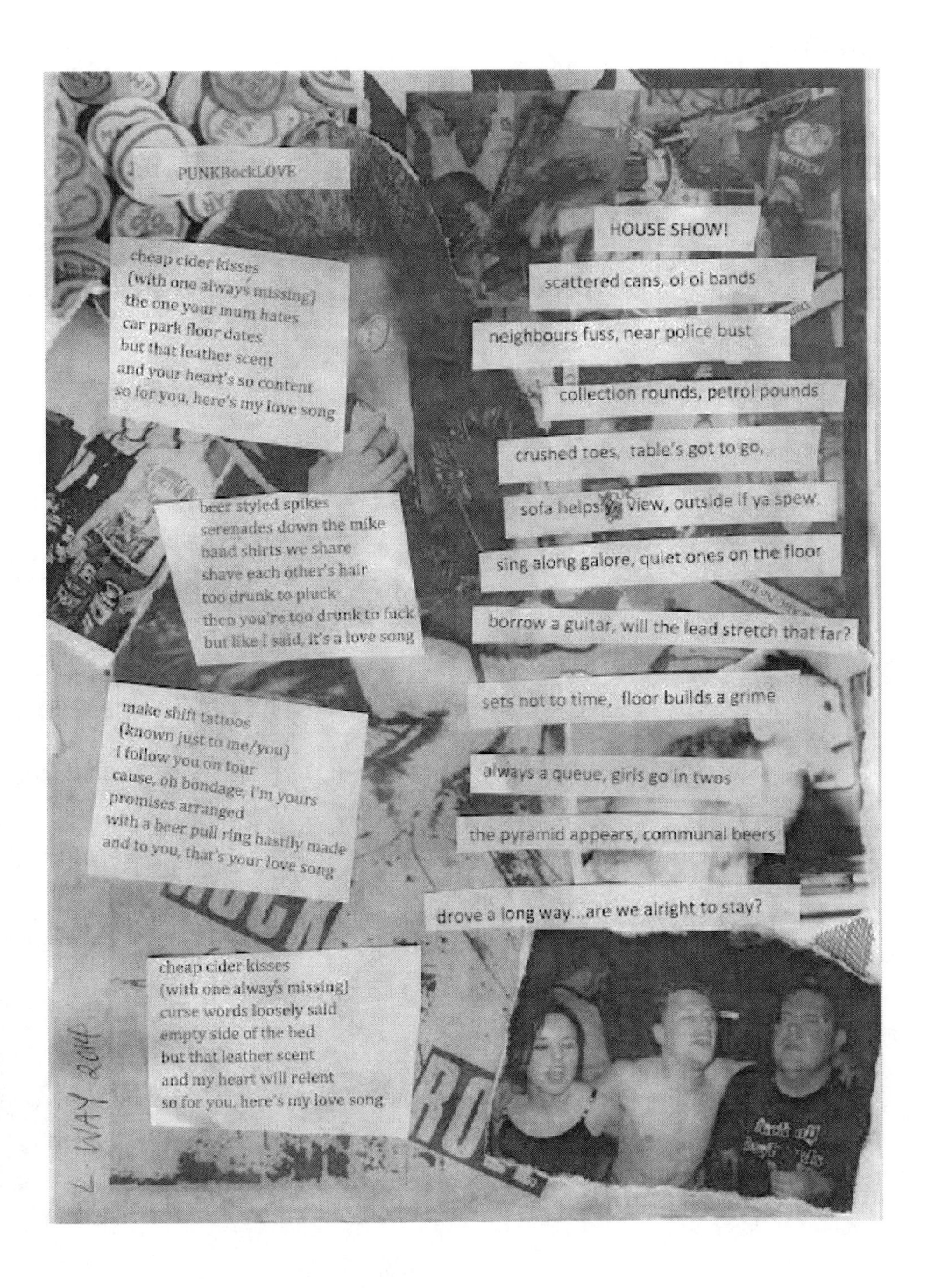

PUNKRockLOVE

cheap cider kisses
(with one always missing)
the one your mum hates
car park floor dates
but that leather scent
and your heart's so content
so for you, here's my love song

beer styled spikes
serenades down the mike
band shirts we share
shave each other's hair
too drunk to pluck
then you're too drunk to fuck
but like I said, it's a love song

make shift tattoos
(known just to me/you)
I follow you on tour
cause, oh bondage, I'm yours
promises arranged
with a beer pull ring hastily made
and to you, that's your love song

cheap cider kisses
(with one always missing)
curse words loosely said
empty side of the bed
but that leather scent
and my heart will relent
so for you, here's my love song

HOUSE SHOW!

scattered cans, oi oi bands

neighbours fuss, near police bust

collection rounds, petrol pounds

crushed toes, table's got to go,

sofa helps ya view, outside if ya spew.

sing along galore, quiet ones on the floor

borrow a guitar, will the lead stretch that far?

sets not to time, floor builds a grime

always a queue, girls go in twos

the pyramid appears, communal beers

drove a long way...are we alright to stay?

you joined a punk band in your teens
you joined a punk band in your teens
dyed the hair, ripped the jeans
metal additions to your face
scribbled anthems about the place
pre-gig drinking, cider to hand
learnt all the lyrics to your favourite band

you joined a punk band in your teens
dyed the hair, ripped the jeans
DIY tours, up and down
joining the scene in that night's town
hurried homework whilst en route
drunken guitarist, amp set to mute

you joined a punk band in your teens
dyed the hair, ripped the jeans
marker remains on your hands
token girl amongst the bands
stolen beer haul, stashed in the kit
the van starting to smell like a dirty armpit

you joined a punk band in your teens
dyed the hair, ripped the jeans
inherited stud belt off ya dad
swearing, farting...honorary lad
week-night drinking, losing at pool
sneaked cigarettes on the way to school

you joined a punk band when you were a teen
dye your hair now so grey can't be seen
bass guitar could do with a dust
band shirt back on, for gigs it's a must
always good when there's a place to sit
grateful when venues are not that well lit
you joined a punk band in your teens
a different size now, but still in the jeans

YOUR THE ONLY ONE WHO KNOWS YOU

What savior is this christ?, our holy redeemer that has saved no-one. Where was his love in 'Northern Ireland', 'El Salvador', when the child was ripped open by bomb and gun. Throughout history its been the same twisted lies by popes, vicars, priests, clergymen and the state that justifies all the wars we've ever had. Seek guidance in christ and you shall have eternal happiness, President Reaguns got a new swimming pool, and a place to hide when the bombs are dropped. Prime minister thatcher's got lots and lots of wealth so she can buy authority with cruise and trident, then tell us its protection(for who?) Hitler, Goebells, Amin tortured millions, they too had christ on thier side. Alister Crowly who called himself the 'beast 666', tortured animals, had rituals and cermonys which led to rape and the the deaths of countless individuals of whom had associated with him. He had the devil on his side(so he claimed). Niether crowley or hitler were the lesser of the two evils, the latter inflicted pain on a lot more people the reason being that he was in a more powerfull position than crowley was. Theres no telling what crowley could have done if he were in the same position as hitler.

From the moment we are aware of things around us we are conditioned by first of all our parents, then school, these two authoritys leave a biased impression of the world we live in and try to mould us into the passive stereo-type that does but never questions.

WHAT GOD SAVED? HAS EVER NO-ONE HAS THE CONTROL RIGHT TO YOUR MIND. THE ONLY T IS YOUR GOVERNMENT SELF

MUST WE BEAR HIS GUILT & SIN FROM THE CRADLE TO THE GRAVE • ALTERNATIVE

Our minds are constantly being bombarded By thier definitions of 'good and evil'. We are told that christ is good and the anti christ is bad, once you regognize this you are told that if you do not believe in christ as your savior you are condemned to the pits of hell What a load of BOLLOCKS! Those who choose to put thier faith in iethier God or the Devil are only fooling themselves, no idol has ever saved. We all have good and bad in us only ourselves can truly know ourselves, not some heavanly figure or forked tailed monster. These manifestations are are inventions of the body which governs us, the sooner we realise this the more chance we give ourselves to run our own lives.

The bible tells some really nice stories, but can you truly believe in a god that condones the dominant man and the submissive woman. GOD made man in his own light. WE'LL its pretty dark in here.

I SEEK NO ONE AS MY SAVIOR, I AM THE ONLY ONE WHO KNOWS ME.............................

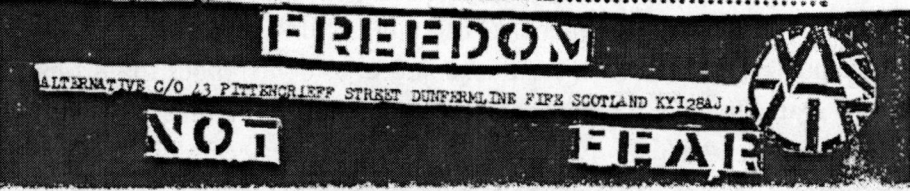

FREEDOM NOT FEAR

ALTERNATIVE C/O 43 PITTENCRIEFF STREET DUNFERMLINE FIFE SCOTLAND KY125AJ

Gig handout by The Alternative

DUNSTAN BRUCE, AND WHY IS HISTORY SO UP FOR ANARCHO-PUNK?

Lucy Robinson – University of Sussex

It has increasingly struck me that all of a sudden there seems to be a lot of anarcho-punk knocking around historians. There have been a number of British academic conferences and events around the politics and aesthetics of anarcho-punk, increasing numbers of academic publications, online resources, documentaries, homages, and the contemporary legacies of anarcho-punk seem to be woven through today's Occupy and UnCut activism.[79] These historical connections are often but not always embodied in the collectively organised band Crass. In the original blogpost on which this article is based I was trying to work through what the implications of this might be – what happens when we start to turn recent cultural resistance into 'history' and what version of anarcho-punk gets churned out in the process.

Every year the British Government releases a set of previously secret documents under the thirty year rule. This year's documents released by the National Archives included papers from 1984 which uncovered the government response to a hoax by Crass who faked and recorded a phone conversation between Thatcher and Reagan about strategy in the Falklands War. The hoax was momentarily thought to be the work of the Argentine or Soviet security services.[80] Although a few individual politicians had questioned the legality of certain military decisions, at the time there had not been much organised formal resistance to the Falklands War. In a context with little explicitly political resistance, cultural resistance filled a gap. The hoax raises interesting questions for historians who are concerned with the limits of subcultural, countercultural or wider popular cultural production as a form of resistance. Debates over the extent to which subcultures, or countercultures, constitute political resistance have been in place since the earliest subcultural studies that came out of the Birmingham Centre for Contemporary Cultural Studies in the early 1960s. It struck me that the Crass hoax put these debates in a different light. When the State responded to a countercultural prank as if it was part of their cold war security forces' stalemate manoeuvres, then academic arguments about the extent to which culture is or isn't related to 'real politics' don't seem as abstract anymore. The recent growth in interest and work on anarcho-punk more generally therefore may also help us to slip through the cracks of the argument about whether subcultures are or aren't really political, and seems to have some real purchase at the moment.

---

[79] See for example, 'No Sir, I Won't: Reconsidering the Legacy of Crass and Anarcho-punk', Oxford Brookes University, June, 2013 numerous successful events organised by the Punk Scholars Network such as The Punk Scholars Network in Association with Cultural Exchanges presents: Penny Rimbaud, DeMontford University, February, 2014. Matt Grimes, 'Musings on British Anarcho Punk', http://www.mgrimes.co.uk/, Alexander Oey, (Dir) *Crass: There is No Authority But Yourself*, (2006), Jeffrey Lewis, *12 Crass Songs*, Rough Trade, (2007)

[80] http://thehippiesnowwearblack.wordpress.com/2014/01/06/thatchergate-tapes-cabinet-papers-from-1984-released/

I'm not going to do a full on secondary literature survey here, but I thought I would just note some of the key texts that have been published over the last five or so years.[81] Just glancing at the places where academic work on anarcho-punk gets published spoke to me of the ways in which we could use it to engage mutually with politics and cultural production: *Journal for the Study of Radicalism, Socialist History, Popular Music and Society,* and *Music & Politics*, for example. Ian Glasper's *The Day the Music Died*, used oral history testimony to weave together a chronology of the networks and spaces that map the diversity of anarcho-punk as a lived identity.[82] Richard Cross's work on Crass suggested to me what it was about anarcho-punk that has helped historians to use it to slip between models of political activism and cultural production more easily than other case studies. 'Anarcho-punk', he wrote, 'lacked the strategic concerns, or the ideological and historical baggage of the formal anarchist movement, but it ignited the interest of tens of thousands of young punks with an anarchism visceral, passionate and angry, and through its insistence that punk rock itself might yet be refashioned into a revolutionary weapon'.[83] Mapping networks, and valuing emotional connections as political experiences, aren't just a methodological imposition on anarcho-punk; they were woven all the way through it. My own Phd research had been informed by George Mckay's work and there are earlier articles on Crass, such as Stacy Thompson's 'Crass Commodities' from 2004, but Cross's article was the first academic article on anarcho-punk that I included on the Thatcher's Britain reading list, and his website The Hippies Now Wear Black is an invaluable resource.[84] As the academic and wider analytical community around anarcho-punk has grown so have the digital connections between documents, posts and articles: so Cross's article is now reposted on the Kill Your Pet Puppy blog, including critical engagement that has helped students position themselves in wider conversation about what is at stake when we write these types of histories.[85] It has also allowed them to think about how it is that set piece narratives develop in historical and memory work – in identifying Crass as a starting point and key case study for the history of anarcho-punk, what other stories are flattened out? And what new set piece narratives are being consolidated? Matthew Worley's work has been key in demonstrating the widespread political and historical significance of taking anarcho-punk seriously. He also resists falling back on set pieces that pretty much replace Crass, for the Pistols earlier work. Instead his work decentred Crass by using Discharge whilst positioning anarcho-punk as part of a wider historical analysis of how the cold war nuclear threat played out at both a global and local level.[86] Pete Dale has pushed the focus beyond the retrospective, to begin the next stage of work on the legacies and events triggered by anarcho-punk.

---

[81] Other earlier texts worth looking out are Tim Gosling, '"Not for Sale": The Underground Network of Anarcho-punk', eds. Andy Bennett & Richard A. Peterson, *Music Scenes: Local, Translocal, Virtual*, Vanderbilt University Press, (2004). Stacy Thompson, 'Crass Commodities', *Popular Music and Society*, 27:3, 2004, 307-322. Brian Cogan '"Do they owe us a living? Of course they do!": Crass, Throbbing Gristle Anarchy and Radicalism in Early English Punk Rock', *Journal for the Study of Radicalism*, 1:2, 2008, 77-90

[82] Ian Glasper, *The Day the Music Died*, Cherry Red Books, (2006)

[83] Richard Cross, 'There is no authority but yourself: The Individual and the Collective in British Anarcho-Punk', *Media and Politics*, Summer, 2010, p2

[84] George McKay, *Senseless Acts of Beauty*, Verso, (1996), http://thehippiesnowwearblack.wordpress.com/, Stacy Thompson, 'Crass Commodities', *Popular Music and Society*, 27:3, 2004, 307-322

[85] http://killyourpetpuppy.co.uk/news/hippies-now-wear-black-rich-cross/

[86] Matthew Worley, 'One nation under a bomb: The Cold War and British Punk to 1984', *Journal of the Study of Radicalism*, 5, 2, 2011.

Dale helps us to start working out why there is so much anarcho-punk knocking around. Dale shows us why we all seem to think that 'anyone can do it' and why we are now investing in anarcho-punk.[87]

All this work, and particularly my students' growing engagement with it, has made me wonder what work anarcho-punk has been doing for us as historians – it seems to be helping us get at something that we couldn't quite get at before. It seems to be getting us beyond some of the traps that we'd got ourselves into when talking, writing and researching about punk. Despite, or perhaps because, of the ever increasing amount of academic and popular history work being done on punk, we'd got rather stuck with the standard hang-ups and largely reiterating a consolidated top down narrative about early (and therefore 'original' punk). So, lots of the discussions have been around whether or not punk was 'authentic', or 'art school slumming it', whether it was 'genuinely political' or just a stylistic affinity. And despite the work of some brilliant female participant observer academics like Helen Reddington and Lucy O'Brien, you would be forgiven that there were really only about four or five women involved with punk and they spent most of their time wearing fetish wear and fishnet tights.[88] The explicit nature of anarcho-punk's engagement with practical acts of solidarity, and theoretical as well as everyday engagement with the politics of sexuality, reproduction, industrial relations and cold war militarism does seem to help us out of the set piece positions beyond statements of style. The question for me is whether or not as researchers will just turn it into yet another series of set piece narratives in the process. Sometimes the contradictions of teaching about punk in a university are, well, crass. We've trashed punk by artificially attaching rigid theoretical and political approaches to it, rehashing nostalgia led tales of authenticity and refashioning it into some form of traditional icon led history topped off with a new set of Dead White European Men. Now we've broken punk, bring on the anarchos and we'll have a go at them.

These contradictions run all through my teaching about anarcho-punk, but so do the creative possibilities. I've been using anarcho-punk as a way of teaching the history of cultural politics, with a focus on the importance of form and aesthetics since I started as a Lecturer at Sussex in 2007. In the masters course 'The Falklands War', we used it to think about the ways in which resistance to the war squeezed through the cracks of what Stuart Hall described as the 'Authoritarian Populism' of Thatcherism. One student on the first year this course ran, John Simpson, picked up on this theme and ran with it, literally to Crass's communal base Dial House in Essex. Reading his term paper on anarcho-punk as a form of historical narrative was one of those teaching moments we dream of – he taught me the pedagogical possibilities of anarcho-punk and what can happen when students really do DIY.

Here is how John remembers what he got out of the research process and how it relates to his career as a journalist since graduating.[89]

"The anarcho-punk reaction to the Falklands War was an opportunity to explore the effect of fringe countercultures on broader society and to capture a period of history as reflected in its art. Music is a

---

[87] Pete Dale, *Anyone Can Do It: Empowerment, Tradition and the Underground Punk Movement*, Ashgate, (2012)
[88] Helen Reddington, *The Lost Women of Rock*, Ashgate, (2007), Lucy O'Brien, 'The *Woman Punk Made Me*', ed. Sabin, Roger, *Punk Rock, So What?*; (Routledge, 1999)
[89] http://www.thetimes.co.uk/tto/public/profile/John-Simpson

valuable primary source for historians, particularly in the form of protest songs, but presents challenges in that it is defined by the audience it reaches and the reception it gets. Punk music was the ultimate in provocative anti-establishment art, and its response to the Falklands was effective. Nowhere was it more evident than in the band Crass, whose song *How Does it Feel to Be the Mother of a Thousand Dead* faced calls in Parliament for a prosecution under the Obscene Publications Act for its attack on Thatcher's motives for fighting the war. The process of writing such a recent history was much like journalism – interviewing musicians, sourcing sales figures and using blogs and other online sources. Though the relevance of such a movement as small as anarcho-punk will be questioned, I think it stands proves and reproves itself as an important reflection of its time – the literal disharmony represents the fury of a disenfranchised youth in Thatcher's Britain and the music captures universal outrage at the futility of many of the deaths of soldiers sent to the Falklands. Writing the paper also gave me the opportunity to repeatedly listen to Shipbuilding by Robert Wyatt, which although it isn't anarcho-punk is probably the best protest song of all time." John Simpson

Anarcho-punk also figures in two courses that I have been teaching and writing about. One is the second year course '1984-Thatcher's Britain', and the other is a third year course 'Post-Punk Britain'. Like a lot of the DIY subject matter we cover these courses are collaborative and experimental. 'Thatcher's Britain' is the centre of new open access re-usable digital archive 'Observing the 80s' that brings together voices of experience of the decade. It digitises three types of evidence, volunteer writing from the Mass Observation Project, oral history interviews from the British Library and ephemera from the University of Sussex's documents collection. It is also freely available as an open educational resource. The project was produced in collaboration with archivists, librarians, and students.[90]

The 'Post-Punk Britain' course is a collaboration between myself and cultural historian Chris Warne. It is a third year Special Subject course and we use anarcho-punk to engage with ideas of the changing spaces of political action, as well as the implications of DIY sources for historians. Recent growth in the use of digitisation and social networking as forms of counter history and history from the margins have helped us access zines and writing that up to now might have been almost impossible for undergraduates to locate. The Special Subject is the course that most of our students choose to develop into their independent dissertation and despite the growth of academic work in the area locating primary sources can still be a problem. Kill Your Pet Puppy provides many of the sources used in that section of the course,[91] as does the Brighton based *Schnews*[92] as well as some of the ephemera from 'Observing the 80s' that was donated by Dunstan Bruce from Chumbawamba.[93] I'm looking forward to adding Tom Vague's digitised zines and writing from 1979 onwards to our reading on psychogeography next year and Matt Grimes' forthcoming chapter on how we should relate the zine to the digital. As Matt Worley pointed out alongside the zines, the production of anarcho-punk records as propaganda, meant that they come with loads of useful texts, graphic design and images to be used as primary

---

[90] http://blogs.sussex.ac.uk/observingthe80s/
[91] http://killyourpetpuppy.co.uk/news/crass-capital-radio-reagan-thatcher-tape-new-broadcast-270184/
[92] http://www.schnews.org.uk/archive/index-001-50.htm
[93] https://docs.google.com/file/d/0Bz-9hs_TdzGPNkdXUjJoQkNkbUk/edit?pli=1

evidence. Alistair Livingston, 'founder-member' of the Kill Your Pet Puppy Website pointed out the relationship between the history we are uncovering and the digital form of the archives we can use. He responded to my initial blog by explaining that the idea for the online archive was itself informed by *The Society of the Spectacle* #157 and is inspired by the idea that the 'act of remembering and recording my/our past was a political act'. Similarly the anarcho-memory boom also helps students engage with the ways in which memoir and memory have helped to structure the resonances of anarcho-punk. Memoirs by both Penny Rimbaud and Steve Ignorant from Crass, and Boff Whalley from Chumbawamba are already on the reading list.[94] The reading list for the course is publically available through the aspire system.[95] We will be adding new memoirs to the list as they get published, for example Viv Albertine's *Clothes, Clothes, Clothes, Music, Music, Music, Boys, Boys, Boys*.[96] The contradictions around new moves to historicise anarcho-punk in academic research, also run through our moves to teach it. Chris Warne and I have been producing academic work based on our reading of teaching as a form of theoretical work.[97] Alongside other 'punkademics', we are exploring the possibilities of not just teaching about punk, but also of teaching as punk.[98] The course is student led, with pedagogical principles and research agendas set by the students. This is all very well in terms of the teaching experiences for us, and students are on the whole positive about our experiments, but it is cut through with contradictions. After all, however DIY our learning modes – we still set an exam, we still mark the essays. I'm hoping that we can see them as creative tensions which allow us to think in more complexity than simply replicated existing power relations but changing the subject matter.

One of our students on the first year of the course, Jake Flynn's dissertation has a particular affinity with the issues I'm trying to work through in this piece, so I thought I'd ask him to add his reflections to it. His subject area is: *There is no better time than the present to be a social historian; using anarcho punk as a means to construct a collective*,

"My dissertation is mainly going to revolve around the relationship between the individual and the collective, and the way that the collective is constructed by both members of the subculture and by the historian. My justification for the use of anarcho punk as a means to unpack this relationship is that they were a subculture that refused to associate itself with the 'system' and resisted being incorporated into the mainstream, both musically and ideologically. Through the use of memoir/autobiography, biography and academic work that has been carried out, I am going to look at not only how anarcho punk established itself as a subculture, but how historians are able to use subcultures as a source of study in order to construct and reconstruct social history. This will all fall into my overarching argument that there is no better time to be a social historian than the present, due to the resources, methodologies and technologies that are now available to social historians." Jake Flynn

---

[94] Penny Rimbaud, *Shibboleth: My Revolting Life*, AK Press, (1998), Steve Ignorant, *The Rest is Propaganda* Southern Records, (2010), Boff Whalley, *Footnote*, Pomona, (2004).
[95] http://liblists.sussex.ac.uk/lists/672DC9ED-8CCB-2AB7-38AD-B58FB2FDE43C.html
[96] Viv Albertine, *Clothes, Clothes, Clothes, Music, Music, Music, Boys, Boys, Boys*, Faber & Faber, (2014).
[97] Lucy Robinson and Chris Warne, 'Investigating the sixties at a sixties institution: teaching as historiography', *Historical Research*, 87, 235, 2014.
[98] Zack Furness, *Punkademics*, Minor Compositions, (2012).

With these strands of memory, narratives, participant observation, and representation in different types of evidence in mind I couldn't resist 'inviting' film-maker Dunstan Bruce and ex-member of Chumbawamba to be part of the 'Thatcher's Britain' course. To be honest, this invitation usually involves me taking Dunstan out for brunch, promising I'll never ask him again if he just does it 'this year', and Dunstan being lovely and saying yes. In the 'Thatcher's Britain' course we pick up on anarcho-punk in our workshop seminar on different forms of resistance, and in the discussion of the Falklands War. Chumbawamba's song on against Clause 28 which prohibited the spending of local government funding on the 'promotion of homosexuality', and the Alton Bill, which attempted to lower the legal time limit to terminate a pregnancy, introduces the lecture on family values and feminism.

Dunstan takes over one lecture every year, shows sections of film projects that he is working on and we go through the history of Chumbawamba in a Q&A format. Although we always pick up on the miners' strike, narratives around 'selling out' by signing to a major record label, the surprising experience of having a hit single with 'Tubthumping', and protesting against then Labour Party Deputy Prime Minister John Prescott who refused to back the dockworkers strike during a bitter year long strike, despite having been himself a member of their trade union. Chumbawamba found themselves alongside Prescott at the Brit Awards in 1998 and one of their number emptied the contents of a champagne ice bucket over Prescott. Apart from these headlines, the format of our sessions is always pretty loose. As a film maker and by virtue of 'having been there' the discussion slips between life history practice (analysis of him and his memories as a type of historical evidence), and cultural commentary (analysis by him from the cultural practitioners point of view). I am delighted therefore that Dunstan has written something for this blog, reminding us that there is more at stake than an academic fresh new market, and reflecting on what he gets out of my 'invitation' to take part in Thatcher's Britain.

"Ever since the inception of Chumbawamba in 1982 we always strove to champion the underdog, looking for stories that slipped through the cracks of history that would counterpoint the accepted version of events. Stories that illustrate the challenge, the struggle, the sacrifice and the small victories won against the odds that show that revolt, rebellion and revolution even, are constantly fermenting, and that there was and still is a culture of resistance.

I'm no academic but when Dr Robinson asked me to come and be part of her Thatcher's Britain course at the University of Sussex, and talk about my own experience of the 80s I jumped at the chance. Here was an opportunity to give my own eye-witness account of the anarcho-punk world I grew up in and then specifically through my experience of the miner's strike of 84/85 how my own political horizons widened massively and how that impacted on the methods Chumbawamba used to try and influence, firstly, the underground and then later, the mainstream.

It's not just a one-way process though as the format of the class gives Dr Robinson the opportunity to input ideas and critique my responses which means that each year there is a new revelation or a new idea put forth, or a new interpretation of a collective decision that the band made. It feels like that the impact of what the band did changes in influence each year as we explore different ideas. And of course, each year I remember a different anecdote that illustrates some long forgotten idea which stimulates new thought on how politics and pop can combine effectively or how individual ethics may be compromised for the greater good.

It's always interesting for me and always challenging; I think the dialogue between eye witnesses and a new generation of interested students is an essential and vital part of us reclaiming history from the accepted norm and helps to give a voice to those whose accounts are largely subsumed in the conventional narrative of accepted history." – Dunstan Bruce.

UPDATE: Since I published the original blogpost Dunstan has embarked on a new and exciting music project Interrobang?. I'm not claiming the two facts are related.

MOLESWORTH

ON TUESDAY 5TH FEBRUARY, 1985, OVER 1500 SOLDIERS AND POLICE FORCIBLY EJECTED 200 PEACE CAMPAIGNERS FROM MOLESWORTH. IT WAS THE LARGEST OPERATION OF ITS KIND EVER STAGED IN MAINLAND BRITAIN. WHY?

THE GOVERNMENT PLANS TO INSTALL, BY 1988, AMERICAN CRUISE MISSILES WITH ENOUGH EXPLOSIVE POWER TO DESTROY 1000 TOWNS THE SIZE OF NORTHAMPTON.

THIS WILL MAKE MOLESWORTH A MAJOR TARGET IN THE EVENT OF A NUCLEAR WAR. HOW FAR ARE YOU FROM THE CRUISE BASE AT MOLESWORTH?

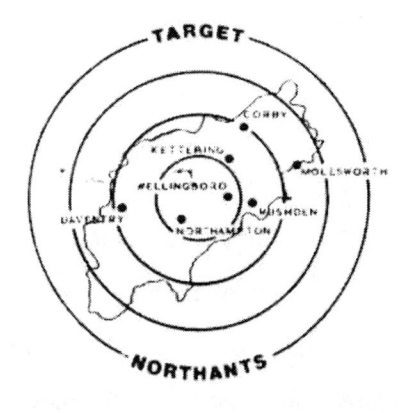

A MAJORITY OF BRITISH PEOPLE ARE OPPOSED TO THE SITING OF CRUISE MISSILES IN BRITAIN. ARE YOU?

DEMONSTRATE
SATURDAY 23RD FEBRUARY
ASSEMBLE 2pm. THE MOUNTS
JOIN US - STOP CRUISE!

Molesworth Demonstration Handout by Persons Unknown

Bottom-feeding on the Crusty Carousel *Martin Cooper*

There is one major stumbling block to me recalling the anarcho punk scene: my memory, or lack of it. To paraphrase: If you remember what happened during the anarcho punk scene you weren't really there. Or, I have the memory of a goldfish after enjoying myself too much in the late Eighties/early Nineties (was that the heyday?) I was preparing to do what I normally do these days: let everyone down and slack off. But Tim Fish (no relation) lent me a copy of Steve Ignorant's autobiography 'The Rest Is Propaganda' and it acted like a literary TARDIS and sparked some memory neurones back to life. Like Steve, The Clash changed my life but it was actually Crass's 'How Does It Feel?' which provoked me to finally pick up a guitar and form a band.

Reading his book, the thing that interested me was that Steve was at the pinnacle of the 'movement', a leader, while I was at the arse-end of the scene. Yet our experiences within that scene seem remarkably similar. As with anything in life when you look back; you only remember the highs and lows. The highs were the wonderful people we met as we trudged up and down the country in a hire van while barely scraping expenses. Salad From Atlantis was certainly a not-for-profit band. We never made any money! But we did it because we loved it. Yet the lows mainly involved people who expected you to behave like St Christopher while sleeping on a concrete floor or in the back of rent-a-wreck, while playing a venue which was a death trap waiting to happen. It shocked me that Steve Ignorant had to put up with some of the things we had to: toilets a Tudor would rebel against, food with cockroaches involved, people living in the ceiling above the so-called venue toilet, yet he should have been at the top of the food chain, so to speak.

Every gig back then seemed to be a benefit. I didn't mind not making money, I just wanted to enjoy myself, but others who had the gall to want to be paid for attracting 200-odd people to a venue in the middle of nowhere were condemned as 'rock stars'. I was happy just to be out there. I never had the chance to go abroad until the first Salad From Atlantis tour of Holland and Germany. I was 21. My first experience abroad was playing The Last Bus Shelter, a Brit-run squat in Amsterdam. We probably played to a dozen people following a 12-hour journey but of those who were there, I still count half a dozen of them as my mates. And that's more than a quarter of a century on. To go from being treated like scum when playing British pubs ("you've done your set, now fuck off") to unlimited beer, smoke and a meal thrown in? Paradise.

A lot of the venues we played in 'mainland Europe' were former Second World War bunkers. Brought up on 'Where Eagles Dare' and Action Man, I thought it was great. We got to play Berlin supporting Blyth Power just after the Wall came down. What the locals thought of these crusties wandering up and down No-Man's Land I don't know. I'm typing these ramblings the day after learning that Blyth bassist and driver Protag died of cancer. On one of the tours we did with them, we became caught up in a riot in Hamburg. We had just arrived at the Flora squat venue in Hamburg when an air-raid siren went off. Punkers immediately donned crash helmets and armed themselves with riot shields and baseball bats. We didn't have a clue what was going on (as thick Inzalafen we couldn't speak the lingo, what, what) but it turned out that right-wing Hamburg SV football fans were attacking the St Pauli fan-led venue. With frightening efficiency, the punkers formed ranks, charged up the street and drove the fascists into a nearby bar, before chucking in smoke bombs and returning to the venue in an anarcho-style victory march. Dashed organised those German crusties.

When we finally ended up where we were sleeping after the gig, there wasn't enough room for the shit support band so we ended up schlafting in Protag's van watching Robocop, running down the battery and then being attacked by wasps in the morning. But we must have enjoyed ourselves, I remember it. Going on numerous tours with Blyth Power who were, again, heroes of mine was a great experience. They were grown-ups to our pathetic schoolboy nonsense. They ate stuffed vine leaves and drank tea. We ate whatever was going and only had eyes for whatever booze was going and, if there were drugs about, yes please and bugger the consequences. Protag was the granddaddy of the grown-ups and I feel even older than ever now I've heard he has gone. To have lived that clean a life (no fags, drugs, booze or meat) and to have died of cancer says something: if there is a God, he's taking the piss.

In fact our childishness is summed up by my two main memories of Protag: dressing his bass guitar with a pair of Tim's skiddy old pants at the end of a tour (the gesture was returned the next time we played together), and accidentally hitting Protag on the head with a baguette while listening to Court Of The Crimson King somewhere in Europe (probably Belgium). The oasis in the UK was the Bradford 1 in 12. Unfortunately, the only time we played there was during a tour with Citizen Fish in which the promoter, obviously not a footie fan, had booked to coincide with the 1990 World Cup. Tim Fish (SFA bass) is blessed with having no interest in footie whatsoever (as a Pompey fan how I wish I had his outlook), but myself and Rolf Johnson (drums) were infected by the British disease. So we used to do very 'un-anarcho' things such as go to footie matches while on tour. If a Bristol City away match coincided with a gig nearby, we'd go to that. If a Pompey match could be fitted in, we'd go with that (and get stick from all angles for having pink Mohawks and the like).

Tim's indifference came to a head when we attended a spicy derby between Swindon and City. Tim tried to feign interest but confused everyone when he seemed to switch sides and cheer on Swindon while we feared we'd get our punkoid heads kicked in by the surrounding City fans. It turned out Tim didn't realise that teams changed ends at half-time. We let him off after that and he tended to sit in the van and read a book if Rolf and I were getting a match in. The Citizen Fish World Cup Wipeout Tour started in Ireland and our first gig, in Dublin, coincided with England playing Cameroon in the quarter finals.

I thought I'd got away with it as the venue had the match on TV at the far end of the bar so I could watch it as we played, albeit on a tiny screen. I always put the audience first: if there was one or 100 people in the room I always gave it 110% (cliché alert), but this was England in the World Cup quarter finals and I'd been watching us being crap since my first match against Poland in 1973. Come on? Then, when the warm-up band started, the TVs were turned off and I thought it was all over. No footie for me. But, just as we were about to go on, the landlord stormed on to the stage and cancelled the gig. Some twats had smashed the toilets (which had only recently been plumbed in) and that was the end of that. "Can I still watch the match downstairs?" asked a selfish twat, and I found myself the only person in a Dublin pub supporting England. Despite that, and being part of the group being blamed for smashing up the bogs, somehow I survived without getting my head kicked in. Revenge rode in shortly after. After beating Cameroon 3-2, England were playing Germany in the semi-finals, and guess who was playing with a German band that night?

So there we were in Birmingham, with the German band at one end of the bar, and Rolf and I at the other. I'd always put the music first but this was England in the semis of the World Cup. This was something I'd waited for since my introduction to English football misery. We had to go on first. But as the match developed and beer went down, the German band and Rolf and I started to mutter at each other in our mother tongues. "You've got to go on now," said the promoter. "No, it's near the end of the match." "Time to go on, NOW." "No, it's extra time." "Right, you've nearly used your whole time up now," "It's penalties!" We had to watch Chris Waddle's penalty soar over the bar, I imagine it is still sailing out in space even now, then we had to go on stage and during the 15 minutes we had left we played the most miserable, slow-motion set possible. Then, we had to stand and watch the German band come on stage and have the party of their lives. Fair play to them, but it hurt. Citizen Fish, sensibly, didn't give a shit.

And so it came to the Bradford 1 in 12 gig which clashed with the World Cup final itself. Myself and Rolf were still depressed but the amazing people we met there pulled us through. Anyway, football was definitely not cool in the anarcho scene, which is why it made me smile to find out that Steve Ignorant was a closet footie fan. Like Crass, we were involved with Southern Records but things didn't quite work out. I was amazed to be invited to come up to London to talk to John Loder after he expressed interest in our second mini-album (we never had enough money to record a full album) that we were looking to release.

The whole thing was a 'concept' (more on too heavily embracing the 1970s later) on Scientology. Taking the piss, basically.

John Loder sat us down in his office and asked: "This track 'March Of The Sea Orgs', what's it all about?" That sent me into a rant, 'These brain-washing fuckers, they only want to sell you books then get your bank account...' John Loder looked me in the eyes and said: 'My wife and I are both Scientologists.' I replied: 'So I don't suppose you'll agree to the album being called 'Who's In The Cupboard? L Ron Hubbard' then?' The mini-album came out as Plastic Paradise as, if I were nasty, a tax loss. But perhaps it was all genuine? We never got anywhere (queue bitterness and spite).

So that's some short, shoddy, shameless anecdotes from the anarcho punk scene. The problem we had was that I always wanted to inject humour into the set and that was generally frowned on. As Steve Ignorant says, the early Crass numbers were full of humour (Heart Throb Of The Mortuary, etc) until the whole scene lost its funny bone culminating in unlistenable paeans such as Yes Sir I Will. It became 'revolution by numbers'. Every band had an anti-Poll Tax song, an anti-Falklands song, an anti-nuclear song etc. There was nothing wrong with that whatsoever, but there needed to be room for other ideas such as Josef Porta's history and trains (Blyth Power) and pure lyrical genius (Mark Wilkins' Astronauts).

When SFA tried to get its first album on Bluurg, Dick Lucas (who is my best mate from the scene by the way) said: "I love the music, but Something In My Cyder, what the fuck is that all about?" Salad From Atlantis was also too open about its influences. We readily mentioned the fact we'd been inspired by

Gong and Hawkwind and, as far as the fanzines were concerned, we'd pissed on our own fireworks from the off, and we were never going to get a good review. Almost all zine review sheets sent back to Southern started off with: "This lot say they are influenced by Hawkwind and Gong, I never got past the first track. Now Fudgetunnel, this really rocks…" Now there's an open mind. We were naive, but there was also an element of, "Fuck you. I know this isn't trendy but it has influenced our sound and I fucking know you listen to it when your mates aren't about." Many other bands were under the same influences, they were just too sensible to admit it. So, when it comes to my memories of the anarcho punk scene, and all those great people I met, and all those wankers who know who they are, to quote England's greatest writer after The Bard: 'It was the best of times, it was the worst of times.'

STOP THE CITY LEEDS~AUG 9th

The first Stop the City demonstration took place in London and was coordinated there by London Greenpeace. It was aimed at disrupting and if possible 'stopping', the workings of the City, the financial centre of London, while at the same time demonstrating against the links between finance and the arms trade and worldwide exploitation.

The demonstration differed from most in that there was no formal organization nor planned actions which the demonstrators would have to conform to if they wished to participate. Rather it was left up to autonomous groups of individuals to pick their own actions and plan and carry them out themselves.

This decision for a flexible demonstration grew out of a need to reinforce protest with direct action since conventional demonsrations were too easily contained, and rendered ineffective, by the police and often, inspite of large numbers, failed to acheive recognition. In effect Stop the City provides an umbrella for a variety of actions and has come to symbolise a united struggle against the system/society that puts profits before people.

Since its conception three Stop the City's have gone ahead in London and regional actions have been planned and taken place to show that the demonstration is not restricted to London - all large towns have their financial centres and share of multinational companies operating in them.

AIMS :

The aim of the demonstration is to draw attention to the overriding importance given to money in our society.

The state and multinationals, as well as many other smaller companies, are continuing to spend vast amounts of money on warfare technology and profit daily from the deaths of thousands of people through wars. August 9 is particularly significant since on this day the second atom bomb was dropped on Nagasaki. Yet today the nuclear arsenal continues to grow and increase its destructive and murderous capability.

In addition, multinationals control the cultivation and export of cash crops from developing countries for processing in the north whilst much of those countries' populations are undernourished and starving. Resources that could be put to use for the benefit of all are stolen and squandered on a wasteful style of living of a small proportion of the world's population.

These unjust power structures are reflected in our own society in sexist and racist attitudes, the abuse of animals in laboratories and factory farms and in the state's response to the miners' demands for control over their working lives - however the injustices are too numerous to mention in any detail in this space.

Finally we must recognise our part in the perpetration of these crimes. At their roots all these issues are linked - the state relies on our compliance, the banks on our custom and the multinationals and other companies on us, the consumer, to buy their shit.

ACTIONS :

The actions are going to take place in and around the city centre, a map of which is shown on the back page. Unfortunately we are unable to give out information about possible targets in case it alerts the wrong people. If you need inspiration, take a look at your nearest town centre and ask yourself what you would go for - the chances are there's one in Leeds. A comprehensive list of shop/company addresses and their locations will be available on the day and there will be plenty of scope for joining in with local group actions if you wish to.

In theory each group with a planned action will be able to mobilise and coordinate other people to take part in or support it, when the time comes. In this way we can be involved in many different actions while only having to organise one or two, or in other words everybody is both an organiser and participant.

Stop The City Handout by Persons Unknown

They May Have Beds, but They Don't Use Sheets *Rebecca Binns*

"It was as though a portion of the population felt obliged to follow some ancient human habit in seeking out some place, however hard to find, where people could build for themselves."
Colin Ward. *Cotters and Squatters: Housing's Hidden History.*

What did opting out of mainstream housing mean for punk squatters in the late 80s? It meant relinquishing a former identity. It involved creating alternate means of financial, social and practical support. It also required creating a communal alternative to the self-interested values driving 80s society. As a conscious choice, for many it invoked hope for change or utopianism. But, for those with the least to lose, it was also a knee-jerk solution to homelessness.

What defined being a punk? Anger, irreverence, subversion, shock…. Punk could be described with any number of adjectives used to denote disparity from the mainstream. But, simultaneously punk was everything that escaped definitions, categories and terms such as these anyway.

Why was squatting part of a punk identity? Without enacting punk in some kind of way, such as this, it ran the risk of become nothing more than a fashion statement or meaningless posturing, easily appropriated for mass consumption; or *Punks on Postcards* as the Culture Shock song claimed.

Such questions hadn't occurred to me before my metamorphosis. I fell into living in a heavily squatted area of North London, as a teenager, in the late 80s, out of necessity. I hadn't even heard of The Exploited, Conflict, Anti Nowhere League or Discharge, let alone 'peace-punk' originators Crass. Growing up I'd noted, but not given much thought to the black clad, dreadlocked audiences at gigs at The George Robey pub in Finsbury Park or squatting the houses opposite my school.

The dominant youth cultural tribe among Londoners when I was growing up were *casuals*. They were into flashy jewellery, designer-name clothes, hip-hop music and break dancing. This was the category I fell into by default before branching out with my newfound friends. The look of dismay on a *casual* and former friend's face who after spotting me in bright orange, winkle-picker boots and dyed black hair, cornered me in the school corridor and said, 'I thought you were like us. Now you're going around with those weirdoes'. I felt sad, but there was no going back.

The like-minded souls I found at school were nostalgic for all things 70s punk. At the age of fourteen, my closest friend, Jo, transformed herself from mousy wallflower to bombshell Blondie incarnate, rejecting the dominant 80s trend for Madonna lookalikes. Our marginal little group would congregate in her bedroom to listen to a constant stream of throw-back punk from the preceding decade: The Clash, The Jam, The Sex Pistols, The Ramones, The Stranglers, The Pretenders, Patti Smith, X-Ray Specs and The Buzzcocks; as well as more contemporary stuff: PiL, The Godfathers, The Cure and Hüsker Du. I revived my love of Two Tone and ska; first ignited when I saw The Specials live at the age of nine. Soon after, Jo got together with the singer from The Senseless Things, who were then emerging as a credible, young, Indie/Punk band. They played a gig circuit around Twickenham and Hammersmith with other Indie outfits like The Milk Monitors and Mega City Four. This was when the term Indie actually meant being independent from the mainstream instead of affecting an alternative look while being simultaneously being signed to a major label. Jo even got to know her hero, Steve Diggle, of The Buzzcocks, when he sang live with The Senseless Things at The Clarendon. We formed our own band that supported them at a succession of venues around Hammersmith around 1986-87. We had myself as the (highly unaccomplished) bass player. That was all fine and punk. Musical ability just interferes with your passion and conviction and all that. Wasn't that the idea?

But the catalyst for becoming a fully-fledged punk-squatter was finding myself homeless at the age of seventeen. I was given the lowdown by a friend and co-worker at the Beigel Bakery in Ridley Rd, Dalston. Over slicing, buttering and filling beigels, Zoe let me know that the flat below her squat was empty. Her boyfriend and veteran squatter, Yannis, had found a way in. We discussed it over dinner at their place. They didn't conform to the media perpetrated idea of squatters at all. On the fourteenth floor of a tower block in Turnpike Lane (later condemned), their home was a respite from the neglectful squalor of the communal walkways and lifts. They furnished, decorated and maintained it with care. In-fact Zoe kept up far higher standards than average, cultivating an extensive knowledge of the merits of various cleaning products on the market; so far, so un-punk. While Zoe worked in the beigel bakery, Yannis was a construction worker and built for it from regular gym sessions. Aside from squatting, they were the kind of people who would have been termed 'decent' by the Thatcher government, which was the first since the Victorian times to create a division between a deserving and undeserving poor. But they were also virulently anti-Thatcher and political about their motivation for squatting; there were no council homes, but an abundance of empty properties. Private rents were too high. They were providing a service to the council by looking after their properties. They also provided a service of sorts to the local residents. Yannis brought home shopping for a marooned old lady living opposite who couldn't make the journey down fourteen floors and across several main roads to the shops. He also helped residents who had no joy with the council maintenance department to fix things up around their homes. This was during an era when there was not even the pretence of valuing community embedded in government rhetoric. 'There is no such thing as society', Thatcher's epitaph for the 80s, signalled an aggressive ideology promoted by her government and implemented by the majority who bought into it.

In August, 1988, Craig and I squatted our first home. Once we had gained entry, we changed the locks and posted a legal notice on the door. It read,

<u>LEGAL NOTICE</u>

THIS EMPTY FLAT HAS BEEN REQUISITIONED TO HOUSE HOMELESS PEOPLE. WE LIVE HERE AND WE INTEND TO STAY HERE. AT ALL TIMES THERE IS AT LEAST ONE PERON IN THE FLAT. ANY ATTEMPT TO FORCE ENTRY OR ANY ATTEMPT TO ENTER UNINVITED IN A THREATENING MANNER WILL BE DEALT WITH UNDER SECTION 6 OF THE CRIMINAL LAW ACT, 1977 AND COULD RESULT IN THE GUILTY PARTY UNDERGOING A SIX MONTH PRISON SENTENCE OR HAVING TO PAY A £2000 FINE. OUR SIGNATURE IS OPTIONAL.

THE OCCUPIERS. HAVE A NICE DAY

We salvaged furniture and a cooker from skips; bringing our own bedclothes and curtains with us. Our home was light and airy with wall-to-wall windows providing a fantastic view across the reservoirs and railway tracks of North London. But, outside the sanctity of our home, the building was a decrepit wreck. The lifts and stairways stank of piss. Often the lights or lifts didn't work. I took care not to meet the eye of most people as attacks and muggings happened on a regular basis. The protracted route to getting anywhere meant journeys for daily essentials were limited.

We survived there without notice of an eviction for the best part of a year. I managed to hold down jobs in the beigel bakery, waitressing and cleaning. Our squat had the semblance of a cared for home. My appearance didn't change that much. I experimented with pink hair for a while. But, for my boyfriend it wasn't just somewhere to live. He was following a dream. His appearance became increasingly dishevelled; dreadlocks cultivated, piercings amassed, rips in clothes acquired. He began to refer to himself (although with his tongue firmly in cheek) as a 'peace punk'. I never heard the term 'anarcho-punk' at the time, although in retrospect this seems to have become the defining label. We came across a huge, squatting, sub-strata community inhabiting a network of streets around Wood Green. We met groups of supportive, enthusiastic squatters who helped us find our feet. Most were in their late teens and early twenties. Some were relative old-timers in their thirties whose jaded appearances reflected the toll of their lifestyle. This community was made up of people from all over the UK, plus a disproportionately large section from Ireland.

People took on low paid jobs, such as street cleaning, where they didn't have to compromise their look, attitude or lifestyle. Some amassed multiple benefits claims and then drank their giros away. Other people refused to sign on as a point of principle; not because they had a moral objection to it, but because they wanted to live self-sufficiently and below the radar of authorities. Others went busking and generally got by on very little money.

We would gather at one another's squat every weekend for a big vegan feast, sourced mainly from skipped ingredients with the remaining costs split between us. Squatted buildings also acted as cafes and venues for gigs with crèche facilities provided. Local punk-squatter bands such as Coitus and Dread Messiah often played. Benefit events to raise money for causes were also common. A network of free festivals in rural locations around the country provided the focus for summer. Otherwise, there was scaling the fence at Glastonbury. We spent the summer solstice of 1989 camping out in the rain a few miles away from Stonehenge. Here, us city squat dwellers joined another group of refugees from 80s capitalism, the peace-convoy, in commemorating the solstice as close to the stones as we could get (the police had cordoned off the area following the notorious Battle of the Beanfield four years earlier).

Among the Wood Green squatters, an Irish couple, Aiden and Kathleen, seemed to adopt the role of surrogate parents. They planned trips for around forty of us to camp out in Hadley Woods. Hallucinogenic drugs led to re-imaginings of our group laughing around the campfire as woodland elves, cowboys, Fagin's delinquents or various other bands of outsiders. One time we were joined by an elderly, bearded refugee from the 1960s; who had clearly had his mind fried by acid. No one knew how he found us. He spouted various insane ramblings, at one point turning to Todd, who was only fifteen years old, saying, 'Hey, I remember you. Hendrix, Isle of Wight Festival, 1970. You were to the left of the stage'; to widespread hysterical laughter. As everyone started to normalise in a jittery kind of way in the early hours of the morning, Aiden and Kathleen had had the foresight to stash bottles of cider up trees. So, we were all involved in a frenzied game of hide and seek; climbing trees to the backdrop of mutterings about the psychedelic sixties from our newly adopted friend.

On eviction, we found a squat among dozens of empties in the network of council estates, which lined each side of Seven Sisters Road, the main carriageway through Manor House. A lot of the estate where we lived was squatted and friends of friends helped us install a makeshift company head to rig us up to electricity. We shared the place with an old friend, Kate, and various others. Craig took to his newly found role as a vegan; preaching to anyone who would listen about the evils of animal products. We were less zealous. Craig was not happy to come home once to find Kate and myself in the kitchen gorging ourselves with sandwiches made with real butter and cheese. It was like going back to school, expecting to be chastised for any transgression. Such types were sometimes called the vegan militia.

Getting on alright. Look after yourself, eat lots of veg, organic is the best, god save the queen, up the IRA, smash the poll tax, never trust a hippy, never give a punk a sip of your cider, see you soon

Scenario-I've loved and been in love with my wife all my life.She's a bit rat now and that as I am myself.Always thought the whole point in life beyond our youthful grace and adrenelin charged flushes was to sit back and smile at this new life we'd created in new bodies.I love my wife asx I sink into her warmth as it folds around me.I feel her firm strong arms which have cradled us all.I sink into deep flesh Iwant to devour.We drift off into our dreams...But, are y you getting enough of it'screamsthe sunday filth I collect with the mail and bring back to bed.Well,never really thought about it.Feels good to me. 'YOU'RE NOT NORMAL.YOU'RE UNDERSEXED AND INADEQUATE'Oh sh it. 'SEXY =YOUNG,STOCKING CLAD CASH,FLASH AND STUPID'. Is this you?if not it's inevitably what you want to be' is it? oh shit,and so on.

"We're on top of the world. I'm insanely excited for no particular reason. Ithink it's combination of escaping the squalor of Manor House,my expeatant child who's reassuringly itting the boot in every few minutes and still being a teenager (just).Sam's fiddling with ndless collection of facial piercings in an attempt to conform her face to normality,no chance

108

My relationship with the police found a new kind of bearing. As an unthreatening young woman, I had never been any kind of target. Now I was increasingly being exposed to a different side of law enforcement. One particular incident stands out when a group of us went to London's Astoria to see Bad Brains play. With us in the queue outside was Ciaran; a slight, softly spoken guy from Northern Ireland. Without warning he was dragged away and forced down a side street by several police. I ran after them shouting, asking why they had taken him. They tried to get rid of me. I could see they were getting psyched up so I followed them. When I arrived at the van, several of them were laying into Ciaran inside it. The force with which one of them hit him was so extreme. He looked completely psychotic. I flung myself in the van screaming a fantastical story that my dad was a Detective Constable in the Birmingham police force and they had better stop. I refused to leave. To my amazement it worked. They let us go. But, it affected my view of the police for life.

People were frequently arrested on spurious charges on the basis of how they looked. It got to the point where police would turn up at the door and ask if so-and-so lived there. We would automatically say yes, assuming it was a friend using an alias name or address. It became an increasingly 'us versus them' existence.

Diary entry, December 1989

...'Who said I didne live here?' screeched Reenee walking in; her little legs in fishnets over blue shiny tights. 'Me and Eimear have only just got out the police station because somebody said I didne live here' she carried on screeching, obviously pissed. 'Good God, could you turn it down about a thousand watts like' muttered Fergus, sticking his fingers in his ears, grinning like a psycho. That set Kate and me off cackling and then Heather joined in and everyone else sat with their fingers in their ears. 'Fucking hell, the three witches of Macbeth or what!' muttered Fergus smirking, his eyes nearly popping out of his head. Reenee continued with her story. 'Normally such a nice, quiet girl' Fergus muttered pulling the pillow over his head as Reenee carried on regardless. 'Is your false name Kimberly Mc Colins?' I asked her. 'Aye, some bastard said it wasn't me'. 'No, I answered the door to them and said Kim does live here', I said. 'Oh well, they're lying bastards then' she decided.

The way people looked became increasingly dishevelled, tattooed and disfigured. The more extreme among us would cause people to scarper when walking down supermarket aisles. They became some kind of haunted species who were referred to by many as scum. This appearance barred many of our group from any sort of employment. So, as buskers, and then increasingly as beggars, they were subjected to 'Get a fucking job' type comments, harassment and beatings.

I remember this poster on the wall of our friends' squat in a burnt out council flat opposite ours. Its powerful message roused ambivalence in me. On the one hand I was taken in by the idea of creating freedom and refusing pre-ascribed versions of reality involving dead-end jobs. On the other, I was scared at the thought of inertia implied by a woman who slept all day. Rather than liberty, was this just a self-imposed imprisonment? I rebelled against the apathetic existence I was afraid of; waking hours before anyone else and sketching them in their sleep. I left the squat one day to find a group of fearful old ladies huddled around the door. We chatted and they said they were concerned to see my lot out drinking on the green to the point where they passed out paralytic. *There were kids around…. they were leaving rubbish all over the place…* Instead of being defensive, I found myself wanting to make them feel better. I apologised. I told them I was off to work. They asked where and I told them about my cleaning job. They were effusive, 'Nothing wrong with that… You're alright girl… It's not you we're bothered about' and so on. I felt sheepish at the flicker of pride, which ran through me.

There was a shift from the healthy DiY attitude set by Kathleen, Aiden and their lot to extreme alcoholism and drug use that infected many Manor House squatters. No one wanted to cast judgement or tell anyone else what to do as this wouldn't have been very anarchic. *It's Up to You* was the mantra (as The Specials had sung). But, as such nihilism (of a seductively enjoyable kind) took hold; it became more and more difficult to resist this particularly toxic form of group-think. Being so young and often without parental homes to go to also made many of us especially susceptible to this kind of peer pressure.

I benefited from being physically unable to keep up with the alcohol and drugs consumption and not having an addictive personality. Still, the lifestyle was taking its toll. I had septicaemia and other signs of malnourishment. My appearance became more and more shoddy. We were evicted and had to move squats every couple of months and it became harder to control who and how many people we lived with.

It was at this time I realised I was pregnant along with several other women in our community. Our friend, Dee, who shared a squat with Aiden and Kathleen had just had a baby. She was enormous at seven months' pregnant when Greig fell for her; nurturing, massaging and caring for her in the months leading up to and during the birth. He delivered the baby himself at their squat without a midwife. When Kate and me visited, after the baby was born, we were offered nuts, raisins or seeds from the bowl being passed around. Then Greig appeared in the room carrying a little frying pan. 'Would you like to eat some of the after-birth?' he said. 'Eeeeeeew! No! I thought you were meant to be vegan?' we howled. He shrugged, 'It's meant to be really good for ya!'

Tales From The Punkside

No 01006 MMR MUSIC Presents
DISCHARGE
Plus U.K. SUBS
SUNDAY 17th NOVEMBER 1991
at THE ASTORIA THEATRE
157 Charing Cross Road, London, WC2 0E
TICKETS £7-00 ADVANCE
DOORS 7-00

UNIVERSITY OF LONDON UNION
MALET STREET, LONDON WC
RIVERMAN & ULU ENTERTAINMENT PRESENT
Poison Idea
HARDONS
PLUS SUPPORT
WEDNESDAY 27TH MARCH 1991
DOORS OPEN AT 7:30 p.m.
IN ADVANCE £5.50
TICKET NO 00626
NO RE-ADMISSION
ADMISSION RESERVED
ON ENTRY

MMR MUSIC Present
A PUNK EXTRAVAGANZA
featuring: Anti-Nowhere League,
Peter & The Test Tube Babies,
The Lurkers and Guests
at THE ASTORIA THEATRE
157 Charing Cross Road, London, WC
SUNDAY 2nd FEBRUARY
TICKETS £7.50 ADVANCE/£8
DOORS 7.00PM

ACADEMY
JUKE JOINT PROMOTIONS PRESENT A TRIBUTE TO
211 STOCKWELL ROAD
1945 — BOB CALVERT — 1988
HAWKWIND
DOCTOR & THE MEDICS · GAYE BYKERS ON ACID
THE PINK FAIRIES · PSYCHEDELIC · JACK LUKAS
MAN · HERE & NOW · THE STAR GHLLS
NIC TURNER'S FANTASTIC ALL-STARS
ATOMGODS · PIGS ON SPIKES

Metropolis Music Present
★ ★ ★
BAD BRAINS
★ ★ ★
Electric Ballroom, 184 Camden High St, London NW1

The Underworld
174 Camden High Street, London NW1 0NE
(Opposite Camden Underground)
Over 18's Only
SATURDAY 17th DECEMBER 1994
RIVERMAN presents
SNUFF
Doors 7.30pm
Curfew 10.30pm
£3.00 advance
Tel: 071-482-1932
ROAR

Metropolis Music Presents
★★★★ 1987
★★★ **D.R.I.** ★★★★★
★★★ ★★★★
Friday 2nd October at 7.30pm
THE CLARENDON HOTEL BALLROOM
HAMMERSMITH BROADWAY, LONDON, W6
Tickets £5.00

No 021

Kathleen went one step further in the goddess stakes with the birth of her baby. When she went into labour, Aiden went out to try to find a working phone box to call an ambulance. But by the time it arrived she had delivered the baby herself and was contentedly breastfeeding him. The ambulance men were astounded. She was nineteen years old. When she found out she was pregnant, herself and Aiden had frantically saved from several income streams and managed to put by £20,000 by the time Oisin was born. They used the money to buy a vast plot of land in Ireland, with several dilapidated buildings and wild horses roaming it. It was going ridiculously cheap before the Irish property boom of the 90s. They did all the work renovating the dilapidated railway signal box and outbuildings themselves. As for me, I continued squatting until around six months into the pregnancy, when I was evicted again.

Diary Entry, January 1990

In one day my whole life is upside down and inside out. I'm like a machine being forced into a new, different stage of my life whether I want to or not. I'm homeless because yesterday without any warning the bailiffs and police came around and did a clear out of Manor House. I can't be bothered to go into details or moan about it. At the time I just burst into tears and cuddled up to Fergus in Finsbury Park. Everything I own from maternity clothes and personal diaries to TV, cooker, record player and baby stuff is in there. I can't get it out until sometime next week, which is very likely to be too late as the whole of Woodberry Downs Estate knows it's empty. I don't see how it won't get robbed...

I was increasingly feeling the pressure of what was becoming a dystopian existence around me. Friends were diagnosed with cirrhosis of the liver or hepatitis. My Aunt offered me a room in her house until I got a hostel place through the council. I said no at first. But she persisted, assuring me she was offering because she really wanted me to stay and it wasn't charity. I wouldn't have been able to take up her offer without the support of people around me. Everyone said I should take the best option for myself and the baby. I missed being the centre of all the action, but was thrilled at having some security. Anyway, I could never get used to putting my feet up and still made it down to Manor House to see people. Once my son was born, I brought him with me to festivals or to stay over in friends' squats for the night. A couple of years later we were settled in a council flat. I was offered a place at art school.

As the years went by, news periodically went round of another person from our group who had died. From a community of around twenty eight people I squatted with as a teenager, ten died from alcohol or drug related deaths, mostly in their twenties. One of these deaths was due to an unprovoked attack while the victim was drunk and unable to defend himself.

Is this then the legacy of the punk-squatters scene of the late 80s/early 90s? What led to the utopia many sought ending in something that seemed closer – to outside eyes at least – to a dystopian nightmare? There was never a plan anyone followed on how to live. The alternative life people created threw up dead ends, but also new beginnings. Many evolved into what the media termed 'New Age Travellers', taking to the road in vehicles with their self-styled families. Did these new beginnings have any value given the disproportionately high number of casualties? I could point out the number of people who have gone on to lead what could be termed 'positive' lives. Some went to university, held-down jobs or branched off into entrepreneurial activities. There are artists, paramedics, social workers, teachers and qualified doctors among them. One even married a policeman. But to define this as 'positive' would be to qualify success in the same mainstream terms people often wanted to avoid. Instead, it should be asked whether there was any point in living an alternative life for the sake of it. Not in terms of how eventually people measured up with the rest of the world. I personally went through an irreversible change through experiencing life outside the usual parameters. As well as being a lot of fun, my 'misspent' youth gave me breathing space in which to reconsider life. As current legislation and policies mean that housing options for young people without means are stifled in ways never experienced in my lifetime or that of the previous generation, it seems apt to reflect on a time of relative freedom. This experience seemed to have been living what punk signified rather than experiencing it vicariously, which would have been no substitute at all.

Becky Binns, 2014

Credits:

Additional photographs courtesy of Nob
Gig tickets courtesy of Mik
Senseless Things flyer designed by Daniel Bennett

Title taken from lyrics to 'Dirty Squatters' by Zounds

To protect privacy some names have been changed

Gig Handout by Mark Davess

"I bunged it together for a laugh as a little handout to give to people in the pubs in addition to the flyer that Alan Smith made (which exists in 2 versions, one without Deviated Instinct, because they got on the bill later, and one with)" – Mark Davess

Crusty *Robert Dellar*

Luke plucked the needle out of Olly's neck. The artist wiped the skin of his canvas with an old J-cloth already sodden with a sticky mixture of blood and ink, and took a swig of his breakfast brew.

"It's all done now" he said, holding a stained mirror so that Olly could admire his reflection. It wasn't a pretty sight. The image confronting him was a mess of black and bloody streaks, the decorated areas puffed up and sore. But his traumatic experience under the needle would be worth it in the long run, because once the skin settled down he'd have lovely blue waves and spirals tattooed all over his face and neck.

Olly cracked open his second brew of the day and treated himself to a generous hit on it. It was a summer's morning at the site in Stanmer Park. Tattooed faces were all the rage in his community, indeed, a mark of distinction among the tribes generally. His new fashion concession would be a welcome bonus to his pulling-power, in terms of womenfolk and also his record-buying public.

Olly was down and out, yet he was up and coming following his decision a year previously to drop out of the local college. On the one hand, he was a tattered and filthy mess bent on self-destruction: a twelve tins of brew a day man with more than a passing fascination with needles which manifested itself in narcotics as well as tattoos; a man who hadn't washed or changed his clothes for months. On the other hand his band, the Revellers, were the hottest new musical property on the crust circuit, an outfit just signed to a major multi-national record company, and poised to shoot from local fame straight up to the big-time. Their jolly repertoire of anarcho-pagan punk struck a chord with tribespeople in Brighton and beyond: it reached out to no-hopers everywhere. Fame beckoned, and the coming evening's show at the old Pavilion Theatre, recently closed down due to withdrawal of public subsidies and then squatted by entrepreneurial anarchists, promised to consolidate the band's growing reputation. Olly sang, strummed, and wrote original material for the band, and his slice of the gate receipts would see him all right for gear and brew for a good few days.

Olly hadn't quite graduated to fully-fledged junkie status and wasn't even truly reliant on his juice, but he was working at it. The more drug dependencies you had on the tribal scene, the more credibility points you scored. Most of Olly's income went on brew and smack, though a regrettable availability problem had moderated his use of the latter, slowing the rate at which his habit developed.

Draining the last of his brew, Olly picked up his guitar and stepped from his trailer into the sun outside. He looked around at the battered unroadworthy trucks, caravans, decommissioned hearses and psychedelically-decorated ambulances and ice-cream vans that sheltered the tribe from the elements. They called themselves travellers, though their existences usually wore a pallid, sedentary complexion. Spending their lives stealing, getting drugged up and fucked up, and poncing money from passers-by in the street, the members of Stanmer tribe were living outside the system, conforming to their own anarchist regulations.

Olly clocked the gaggle of crusty squaws slouched beside a broken-down customised hopper bus. As usual, they were passing round a flagon of cider and sewing beads into each other's locks.

"Like my tattoo?" he asked proudly.

The anticipated approval came as a chorus of whoops and cheers.

"Fancy a shag?" he suggested to no-one in particular, taking off his trousers.

"Only if you play us a song" said Candy, who figured that it was her turn out of the Stanmer crustettes who entertained Olly on a regular basis.

Trouserless, the politically-correct crust-rocker got out his plectrum and knocked off a crowd-pleasing cover:

*"What now? Now you would destroy the earth,
Dry, the river beds,
What now? Now in your control, birth and death,
Dry, the bodies, incandescent in the heat…"*

The old Cr@ss chestnut struck a righteous chord in the hearts of the audience, and was rewarded with a little ripple at the end. Olly flung his guitar away charismatically like an experienced rock professional. "Now," he said, pointing at a pile of empty beer cans, "what about that shag?"
"If you're quick" said Candy, slipping out of her tattered rags, "I'm off into town soon to beg up enough money to sort me for booze and gear for the day."

Olly removed the rest of his garments and the pair climbed onto the stage made out of old tins. They quickly got down to business while the others watched. The tribe had rejected the repressed trappings of bourgeois morality and operated on strict back-to-nature basis. Public shagging on the site was a commonplace occurrence, and Olly's taboo-challenging and exhibitionist tendencies, which had inspired him to form the Revellers, combined to afford him a special pleasure in performing in front of an attentive audience. The crustettes were augmented by further spectators as word got round the site that Olly and Candy were in action on stage. One observer tipped cider over the harmonic duet playfully, but refrained when others offered verbal reproaches for wasting the precious liquid. The tempo was fast and consistent throughout, a metronomic mantra as solid and accurate as a state-of-the-art drum machine. Not too long a timespan elapsed before the rhythm neared the end of its grooves, and repeated to fade until all was silent. Suitably impressed, the congregation applauded and then dispersed. Some went back to their motors to continue getting wasted, while others went into town to beg, busk, hustle, liberate the contents from licences, and lurk in the North Lanes giving fire-eating and juggling displays in the expectation that tourists would throw money at them. As for Olly, he went to sound-check at the Pavilion to be ready for the show which was the next step on his stairway to stardom.

He woke up the next day and couldn't work out where he was. As the fog inside his brain lifted a little, he remembered that he was supposed to have played a concert the night before. His memory struggled to establish itself as his head pulsated to the throbbing industrial soundscape of a serious hangover. His face stung from its adornment the day before, but his disorientation decreased when he realised he was on the Level, surrounded by tribespeople asleep or stirring. Half a mile from the seafront, the Level had been full of trees until it was levelled by a hurricane in 1987, before he'd moved to Brighton from his native Leamington Spa. He didn't recognise the crustette sharing the battered leather jackets which had passed for blankets for both of them during the hot summer night. But gradually the gist became clearer as scraps of memory began to coalesce. The Revellers had delivered a stunning, raucous set in front of an adoring crew of fellow-travellers. Afterwards, Olly had drunk his rider and then picked up a chick who'd travelled all the way from her site in Shepton Mallet to see him strut his stuff on stage. They'd wandered over to the park with a gang of fans, journalists and other hangers-on. This select audience had been treated to a fine display of public shagging by the crust-rocker and his groupie, a show documented by cameramen whose pictures would accompany the reviews featured in the next editions of the music papers. The band wasn't into the jaded rock 'n' roll tradition of playing conventional encores, but Olly prided himself in being an all-round entertainer who always provided fine value for money. The open display of the amatory arts had been the appropriate chaser to the Revellers' set.

Nagging doubts haunted him. He wanted to live fast and die young. He wanted never to wash as an abstract rebellion against society's mind-warping conformities. He wanted to light his fuse, shoot across space like a sky rocket and burn out into spectacular oblivion like the grand finale of a top fireworks display. It was the only course of action for a man of integrity to follow.

And yet, he was worried about what his mummy and daddy would think.

He hadn't seen his parents since blowing out college: he'd kept away from the upper-class reactionaries who'd forced him to go to public school. But his growing musical popularity made it increasingly likely that they'd read about him in the papers. They'd have difficulty with his tattoos, his public shagging displays, his drug habits and his overall degenerate demeanour. They might even come looking for him, track him down to the site and tell him off, and then all his mates would take the piss out of him. Olly had told the tribespeople that he was the orphaned son of the two last members of an ancient tribe of obscure nomadic druids from the chalk circles. He didn't fancy his family giving the game away, but as he cooked up for a shot with some smack he'd procured at the show, he forgot about the potential embarrassment and drifted into a state of emotional vacancy and inner statelessness.

Unfortunately, even after the hit took effect, Olly still felt some self-awareness. Determined to sort out this problem he got up, dismissed his groupie and wandered to the off licence to pick up a few brews. He pulled the ring off the first, sucked on it deeply, and went to a book shop where he located a volume about dangerous dogs. He sat on a pile of remaindered hardbacks and scanned the pet-owners' manual closely. The stink of months of poor personal hygiene wafted unpleasantly, but he was unchallenged by the intimidated shop assistants who thought that hassling him would only lead to trouble. Olly studied, using an objective method of scientific analysis to work out exactly the most brutal breed of hound to be found, on rare occasions, in the British Isles. Luckily, due to a peculiar negligence in dog legislation, the breed was perfectly legal. Convinced he'd done his homework properly, Olly went to a dog shop where, against the odds and in a co-incidental manner virtually impossible outside the realms of fiction, he found a yapping little puppy of just the kind he wanted: a razor-fanged pitbull werewolf!

Olly knew that such hounds could be trained to kill selectively. Naming the werewolf Kano after a particularly vicious cartoon character, over the next few weeks he used aversion and reward techniques to make the dog mercilessly attack, at the sound of a blast on a referee's whistle, anyone smelling heavily of soap, disinfectant, deodorant or expensive perfume. Although no such individuals existed in Stanmer Park, Olly made life-size dolls out of old rags drenched with fragrant toiletries and stuffed with chewy succulent chunks of raw steak. He was pleased with the result as Kano learnt to identify unnatural smells with a good feed.

During Kano's training programme, Olly played a number of concerts in London and even did a small tour of Britain with his band. The Revellers' first couple of singles were released and they both entered the charts. While he remained loyal to his tribal roots and never considered moving off the land, he exploited his new, respectable music biz contacts in order to procure a more regular smack supply. He also started getting the shakes in the morning prior to drinking his breakfast brew. All in all, he mused one day as he sat outside his trailer, his career was progressing satisfactorily and he felt upwardly mobile. His facial tattoo had settled nicely and was no longer sore. He'd hit the milestone of a full year without having a bath. His stardom and drug habits were on the ascendant. His growing rocking reputation had the crusty squaws falling at his feet wherever he went, allowing him to give as many public shagging displays as he fancied. Life was idyllic, just like an anarchist pagan utopia. He was feeling at one with the land, a part of its permanence and its mystery. He reflected that across strange expanses of time, in numerous incarnations and on several different occasions, he'd been born before.

"Hey. Olly!" came a shout. It was Doug, an eminent man on the earth. "Take a look at my hair!" he demanded excitedly as he extended a thick, muddy, knotted lock from the filthy mat stuck stinking over his head and shoulders and stuck it, putrid, under the rock star's nose.

Olly examined it. Even a hardened dirtbag like himself had to admit that it was impressive.

"It's crawling with a completely new breed of lice that I've never seen before" Doug explained. "Look, those orange and turquoise ones! That means I've got the most different types of parasite infestation out of everyone in the tribe!"

Olly twitched jealously. The tribe had always been competitive about creepy crawlies and skin diseases, and whoever had the most was generally recognised as the chieftain. But he didn't worry about it for long, because Kano had by now grown to adult werewolf proportions. Olly and his hound were due to spend the day in town. The first clean bastard to whom Olly took an instant dislike would be in for a nasty shock.

Walking down the Queens Road from the station to the clock tower, Olly and Kano found no suitable targets. Crusties, old-school tramps and long-term dole statistics of every shape and size littered the pavement, passing time aimlessly as one day went past virtually the same as the next. None were clean enough to warrant a good savaging.

Man and dog took a left up North Street and the atmosphere changed, with more well-off folks wandering in and out of banks and book shops. Kano strained a little at the leash hungrily, but Olly kept his patience, eager to find the ideal target.

They took a right into a side alley and found themselves bang in the middle of Brighton's illustrious Lanes. Tourists, trendies, pop stars, lecturers and businessmen turned their noses up at the man and dog in their midst, their olfactory faculties offended by the evil stench of shit the pair exuded. Narrow walkways separated rows of shops selling bright, exclusive scarves, shirts, ornaments and ear-rings retailing for three and even four figure sums. Olly suddenly felt spoilt for choice as he sniffed at the wealthy odours surrounding him. And then, he spotted Dr. Smiley, the nightclub boss hopping out of Darlings, a nearby coffee house. Smiley was a well-known local entrepreneur with a notorious taste in pungent after-shave. He'd made a fortune in the entertainments business, but refused to let the Revellers play his venues because of their unruly reputation and because they weren't good-looking enough. The rocker wasted no time in getting out his whistle and giving a high-pitched blast on it as he let Kano off the string.

The hound leapt into action. Almost immediately he'd brought his victim savagely to the ground. Bystanders were too shocked to do much as Kano began chewing at the trendy's throat, gorging himself on the thickly scented human flesh. Concerned onlookers were scared to go near the dog, but eventually they found some long ornamental poles and tried to make him desist by giving him a few sharp prods. They needn't have bothered. Kano had already realised that the nightclub owner didn't taste half as good as raw steak, and left most of his meal untouched, scampering after Olly who was making himself scarce to avoid possible recriminations. Olly was proud to have such a vicious, loyal werewolf. The crusty and his faithful friend had exacted tribal justice on Smiley, whose corpse had proven unfit even to be dogmeat.

One morning some weeks later, Olly woke up, had a fix, got an audience together and shagged a crustette, drank a bottle of Jack Daniels, and contemplated his situation in life. The Revellers' popularity and workload had increased. Olly was alternating his habitat between the Stanmer Park site and various posh hotels in London as he spent more time in the capital recording, rocking out on stage, shagging in public and avoiding being interviewed by journalists. His album, "Ashes to Ashes Crust to Crust," had been released to a favourable reception and was being hyped to the top end of the charts. The national media were on red alert, wise to the good copy to be made out of a hard-drinking, smack-shooting desperado who never went near a bar of soap and who preferred his sex life to be enacted in front of a large, cheering audience and recorded for posterity by cameramen. Olly was playing hard to get, refusing to talk to the papers, which only made them even more interested by building a kind of mystique. Griffin, the Revellers' record company, had exploited the interest by booking dozens of top journalists onto the guest list of the band's upcoming show at the Mean Machine in Kentish Town. The label had issued press releases playing up Olly's debauched and unhygienic lifestyle, and the reporters were looking forward to seeing what the fuss was all about.

Meanwhile, Olly had made an arrangement with Griffin whereby he'd get a regular supply of smack from one of the company's executives in return for a reduction in the rate of his royalties. This pleased both parties: Olly had an uninterrupted supply of smack which kept him sorted and happy, while the label had an employee tranquilised and docile enough to do as he was told and fit unprotestingly into their corporate plan for his career. As long as Olly remained convinced that he was subverting the system from the inside, he'd serve the multinational splendidly.

The corporate plan, however, included a sinister element unknown to the muck-coated rock 'n roll scumbag. The Revellers had been busy lately, keeping up to the schedule stipulated in their contract, writing and recording new songs at a prolific rate. Olly's habit wasn't yet so entrenched that the wellspring of his creativity had dried up, although it was bound to happen eventually. The band already had enough material on tape to fill another couple of albums. The label knew that Olly's productive life was limited, and knew too that self-destructing rock stars burnt out over a predictable timespan which could be gauged in advance according to the empirical scientific statistics gathered from previous Griffin signings. But they realised that it was better to burn out than to fade away, especially in terms of shifting units. A dead rock star, cut down in prime as a martyr to rock 'n' roll mythology, was far more attractive a proposition to the paying punter than a living ex-legend who'd lost it. Olly's death was an essential strategy in the long-term marketing of the Revellers' product.

Olly had agreed to attend a press conference on the afternoon before the big show. He was still refusing to talk, but just by being in the same room he could give the journalists something to write about. The office was on the top floor of the inner-city tower block that was Griffin Records' nerve centre, and Olly sat on a comfy chair in a corner, reeking of dirt and neglect, swigging from his bottle of Jack Daniels, surrounded by a flock of crust chicks, and looking at the gang of hacks and photographers assembled in front of him. Some people had accused Olly of selling out by switching from Special Brew to Jack Daniels, but Olly felt that making some concessions to rock tradition was justified in order to avoid the error of merely preaching to the converted. He thought about what he ought to do to keep the reporters, and consequently his record label happy. He kept mute as the scribes fired questions at him. He didn't give a fuck about debate. Refusing dialogue, he got out his guitar and gave the audience an acoustic rendition of an old chestnut:

*"I know
It's only rock 'n' roll
But I like it
Like it
Yes I do..."*

The cover was a more mainstream choice than the Cr@ss songs that padded his earlier sets, but a certain mellowing out was essential if his anarchist messages were to hit mainstream consciousness. Cameras were already clicking wildly, but when the song had finished, it was time for Olly's set to enter a new phase and hit a different kind of tempo. Pulling on his Jack, he looked the groupies up and down as he peeled off his grubby rages. A multitude of crustettes had surrounded the Mean Machine since early afternoon hoping to catch a glimpse of, if not some action with their heroes before the show started. The Revellers' record company had sent along an executive to select the best-looking of the girls and bring them back to the offices to keep Olly happy. Griffin Records prided themselves on how well they looked after their star musicians. Olly deserved to be well-serviced by his pick of the chicks, because after all it was to be the final day of his life.

Olly made his selection. The lucky object of his choice divested herself of her garments, which weren't in a much better state of cleanliness than Olly's. Immediately, they were getting down to business while the reporters took notes and the photographers fought amongst themselves to reach the best spots from which to capture the action. Although Olly had partaken in public shagging exhibitions before much larger audiences, he knew that in the long term, this would turn out to be his most major shag yet, because it would wind up in all the national newspapers.

After a while Olly and his groupie completed their show, which had been predictable but perfunctory. A Griffin executive called the press conference to a halt, and the king of filth was carted off to the Mean Machine in time for the soundcheck. It had been a solid afternoon's public relations. Although Olly hadn't compromised his anti-corporate principles by condescending to speak to journalists, he'd at least given them top quality visual footage which would nicely spice up the obituaries in tomorrow's newspapers.

Later, all of the Revellers were in their dressing room waiting for the support band to finish, drinking their rider and shagging some groupies. They needed to give a star performance to book their tickets to immortal rock stardom, but Olly was uneasy. The normally reliable Griffin executive responsible for keeping the smack supply rolling had been due to arrive with the latest batch during the soundcheck, but there was still no sign of him. The others in the band and the assembled hangers-on weren't fully-fledged junkies and couldn't help Olly out. The bandleader had become so confident in the executive's ability to deliver the goods that he hadn't bothered to check out alternative contacts in London.

Already he was getting the early warning signs of a serious cold turkey.

By the time the curtain call came, Olly was shivering uncontrollably and had an aching, longing feeling in the pit of his stomach only partially blunted by the copious quantities of Bourbon he'd ingested. He took the stage with his guitar and started to go through the motions, but his heart wasn't really in it: all he wanted was a nice big fix. Most people in the audience didn't notice Olly's disengagement, but some of the hack reporters saw grounds for criticism. They'd expected degradation and mayhem, but somehow the set sounded flat and Olly seemed twitchy and awkward, not the confident and commanding crust-rocker they'd expected.

The Revellers were three quarters of the way through their set when the executive drug-pusher finally arrived at the venue. He'd scored some extra-special happy powder which was to most smack what Special Brew was to ordinary strength lager. Griffin Records figured that a live overdose on stage was just what Olly needed to consolidate his career. The pusher cooked one up ready for Olly to fix between songs. He loaded the barrel of the hypodermic with a lethal dose of the narcotic medicine. Having been left to sweat it out for a bit, Olly would be desperate to spike up whatever he was given. It was time for the fucker to die!

The executive appeared behind an amplifier, waving the deadly syringe discreetly from a certain angle so that Olly alone could see it. By now Olly was dying for a hit. As soon as the song finished, he leapt across the stage and snatched the needle eagerly. Without waiting for the expected outcome, the executive disappeared and went home, not wishing to be implicated in the ensuing tragedy. Olly shook uncontrollably with greedy anticipation as he made ready to empty the serum into his mainline. Without taking off his guitar, Olly jabbed at a vein a couple of times and discovered that more haste led to less speed, as half of the smack squirted accidentally into the knotted length of string that served as a crusty guitar strap. A third stab at the vein, and he found just what he'd been looking for, squirting the remaining precious serum straight into his bloodstream. Sucking thirstily on the string in an attempt to mop up some of the spillage, Olly staggered back to his space on stage.

The band blasted into the final number of their set. Olly had trouble getting the words out and hitting the right notes from the start. By the second verse, he was just standing there swaying, adding no creative input to the sound whatsoever. As his sidekicks hit the middle-eight, Olly went blue, collapsed and started to gurgle. Loud cheers came from the audience: this was more like it!

The other members of the Revellers were experienced members of the counter-culture and knew exactly what to do in overdose situations. They got hold of Olly and beat at his chest a bit, stimulating his heart muscles. They grabbed him by the shoulders and dragged him round the stage while shaking him up and down, hoping to get his muscles moving and in turn his heartbeat to start up again. It worked. Olly was nicely revived, much to the disappointment of his record label. However, the spectacle had been an exciting finale to the show, and at least wouldn't harm the band's career.

Predictably, the newspapers had a field day about Olly's overdose, and encouraged by Griffin they ran lurid stories about it accompanied by photographs of public shagging. The media coverage alerted Olly's mummy and daddy, who were concerned about their son and unhappy about the trouble he was getting himself into. After the show, Olly had booked himself into a hospital as a precaution. Within a few hours, his parents arrived on the scene all the way from Leamington Spa. They weren't too keen on his facial tattoos, and even his records weren't their cup of tea, but they were ready to forgive him and offer appropriate parental support. Griffin were unhappy that Olly was still alive, but decided against another murder attempt for the time being, figuring that if they pushed it too far too soon, it could backfire.

"We still love you, Oliver" said the crusty's mummy as she stood beside his hospital bed. "Even though you're clearly a drug addict and an alcoholic, you'll always have a room waiting for you in our house. Come back home and we'll pay for you to have special treatment in the finest private drug rehabilitation unit in the whole of the Midlands!"

Olly wasn't in a fit state to argue. Within minutes his parents had discharged him from the NHS bed and whipped him off to an exclusive unit in Leamington Spa. Once he was there, his withdrawal symptoms kicked in with a vengeance and it wasn't long before he was crawling up the walls, scratching, puking, hallucinating, and experiencing the worst aspects of the rock 'n' roll nightmare.

The nurses in the plush upper-class ward weren't happy with the smell that Olly was exuding. He was still refusing to wash, and although his parents were paying over the odds for his bed, it was getting on the staff's nerves.

Olly's mates were concerned about him. At first it seemed as if he'd disappeared off the face of the earth. Rumours were even circulating that an unwise further fix had done him in for good after the gig, and that he'd secretly been buried at a low-key funeral. However, after a little research, crusties from the Stanmer Park site pieced together the truth. Although they weren't pleased about being misled as to Olly's origins and upbringing, they still held him in high enough esteem to forgive him. They knew he was going through a hard time, and resolved to do something to cheer him up.

Olly was causing a right nuisance on the normally placid hospital detox ward. Normally, people brought into detox in Leamington Spa weren't really casualties at all, but merely upper-class hypochondriacs getting paranoid about their habits of drinking a couple of Martinis each evening as a nightcap, and looking for an excuse to be waited on hand and foot for a few weeks in a palatial environment. If the patients had the money to pay for it, this arrangement suited punters and staff at the hospital alike. But Olly was a different kettle of fish. He was going through genuine symptoms of cold turkey from both booze and smack. He'd trashed the ward a few times, and that was bad enough. The smell of him was pissing off the other patients and making everyone feel sick. When an enterprising crustette tracked him down to the ward all the way from Shepton Mallet and got roped into a public shagging display right in the middle of the day area in front of all the other patients and several of their visiting posh friends and relatives, it was the last straw.

Olly's mates had managed to hitch-hike from Stanmer Park to Leamington Spa. They knew he'd be pleased to see them. To give him a nice surprise, they'd brought with them two things which he'd find particularly uplifting: his guitar, and his dog, Kano.

It took the six hardest nurses in the hospital to pin down the young Lord Oliver Fynes-Clinton. The errant aristocrat struggled fiercely, so they gave him a shot of Largactyl to calm him down. The stench was almost unbearable as they ripped off his clothes, but they were determined to see the action through. Using rough flannels, scrubbing brushes and a variety of industrial detergents, they scraped away at the layers of the crusty's filth until, arduous hours later, he was as clean as a whistle. To complete the effect, they sprayed him with choice expensive perfumes and deodorants until he smelt like a reformed character. Then they incinerated his clothes and dressed him in a designer pink fluffy dressing gown from Harrods.

The gang of crusties burst into the ward, dog-handed. Security had tried to stop them, but they'd fought their way through. Staff and patients alike were shocked and frightened by the sudden invasion of scumbags. The ward manager hit the panic button on the wall, which triggered an alarm system designed to alert staff throughout the hospital that all available manpower had to be diverted to the detox ward to sort out an emergency problem. The alarm, a high-pitched wailing, sounded very much like an extremely protracted blast on a referee's whistle. This was too much for Kano, who broke free from his string and made for the sourced of the cleanest smell on the ward. Seconds later, Olly was being savaged mercilessly by the vicious werewolf, whose claws and razor fangs cut deeply and nastily into his face, neck and chest.

Before anyone could do anything, the crusty had expired.

He became a legend, a martyr to the immortal spirit of rock 'n' roll.

Steve Ignorant – Crass – by Jacky Smith

Not Just Boys' Fun (with apologies to 7 Seconds) *Sarah Attfield*

The route to music fandom isn't usually smooth. It's quite hard to map the journey to a love of a particular kind of sound. It's an accumulation of exposure to different music via friends, family, random snippets heard on the radio, TV, in films. It's unlikely to be sudden, but there maybe a catalyst. Maybe a gig that a friend persuades us to attend, or a mix tape gift? In my case it was a combination of a desire for music that really made me *feel*, and a mix tape that introduced me to music I didn't know existed.

Memory is unreliable, and mine is particularly so. I don't remember exact details but I do remember how things felt, the smells, and the sounds – a sensory impression of time and place. So no doubt this recount is all confused. There may be 'history' that I get wrong. I'm quite happy to be corrected. But these memories are real to me and I can still feel the gigs in my body (it's hard to shake off super-fast drumming pounding through the chest). I can smell them (they were pretty pungent – unwashed moshing, beer sodden youths!), I can definitely hear them (ringing in my ears more than 25 years later).

With this disclaimer in mind, here is my attempt at a chronology of experience (which might be somewhat tame compared to the anarcho and crusty punks' tales of anarchy and chaos!).

My exposure to British punk in the late 1970s was limited to what was heard and seen on the television. I was too young for the Sex Pistols et al and in my neighbourhood reggae was the dominant sound, playing across the estate, speakers facing out of windows in the summer. The limited record collection in my household consisted of Frank Sinatra, Perry Como, Neil Diamond, Ella Fitzgerald and then (after the joy of rare birthday money) the Muppets, the *Grease* soundtrack and an album of TV themes. Not a lot of subcultural capital in that lot (I still have them all though).

At primary school we were supposed to like the Bay City Rollers. Girls tied tartan scarves to their wrists and swooned at the mullet-adorned boys in the band. I thought this was rather annoying and didn't join in. At high school we were allowed to like jazz funk or soul. I didn't know what either was and pretended to listen to whichever one seemed to please the interrogator (same when asked on the street what team I supported, being on the cusp of Arsenal/Spurs territory). I didn't listen to Michael Jackson, Level 42 or Shakatak. I quite liked Duran Duran and found Supertramp, 10CC and the Everly Brothers interesting (courtesy of a friend's parents' record collection). I thought the Specials and Madness were cool and wanted to be a two tone girl (although I didn't know what that meant). I probably would've liked soul if I'd known what it was. It was all rather confusing.

An older cousin introduced me to the music of David Bowie and I fell in love. I kept this secret because my friends already thought I was becoming a bit strange. Somehow, Bowie led to Japan, Bauhaus and an array of arty alternative bands. I discovered the Velvet Underground, the Cure and Echo and the Bunnymen.

Musical Society (part one)

1984

Echo and the Bunnymen

spare us the cutter

but I can't spare what's

about to come up

the security thug drags me

from the black-hair-gel crowd

and I swing into the foyer

land full pelt on the program stand

spew my evening's entertainment

over glossies of McCulloch

almost miss my best pointy buckled shoes

grab Suzie

catapult into the street

don't remember getting home

only the bitterness of vodka on my breath

it was Suzie's 18th birthday

she reckons we had a great time

I was sixteen

Then Marc Almond became the thing. I loved this stuff and harboured a working class fantasy of going to art school and moving to Paris.

Goths Night In (Walthamstow)

Soft Cell on the turntable

It was the morning after the month before

and I was looking like a nose with eyes

But the song doesn't match our mood

of sangria inspired

look what we can do!

And lists

making lists

of who to put against the wall

all that needs to be done

but only by us

Trying to understand anger

through backcombing hair

black eyeliner

lurex and studded everything

Just one night

no giving in!

until puking

on the fluffy bathroom mat later

forgetting about the promise

but still listening to Marc Almond

All that shines may not be lamé

This fantasy was replaced with the reality of full-time work in retail after finishing school and the romantic notions of running away with an androgenous cravat-wearing boy started to fade quite quickly.

It was the 1980s and it wasn't nice. Massive unemployment, Thatcher's war on the miners, her war on people like me (council estate kids) made us angry but despondent. There didn't seem to be much we could do, everything was against us. In about 1987, while working in the shop, a boy gave me a mix tape of (mainly) American hardcore bands. I didn't know who they were, but he seemed to think I'd like them so I gave it a go. I loved it. The energy, the speed, the anger, the fun, I was hooked. The bands on the tape included Black Flag, Minor Threat, Embrace, Bad Brains, 7 Seconds, Gang Green, Squirrel Bait, Hüsker Dü, plus British hardcore from the Stupids (I still have my Stupids cap) and some anarcho-punk from the Subhumans (probably the most explicitly political band on the tape and I listened to their lyrics very carefully).

I went along to a gig with my new friend (Ol). I can't remember who we went to see first, but one gig became a few and I ended up seeing lots of live hardcore (and some anarcho-punk, grindcore and thrash). The American bands visited London and played at places like The Clarendon, The Town and Country Club and the Sir George Robey. The venues were all pretty scuzzy back then (and a lot of the old places are no longer around). Sticky floors, repulsive toilets, scary dark corners. The bands were always fast and loud and the ringing stayed in my ears for hours afterwards. We drank loads of beer and we got to talk to the bands sometimes.

Musical Society (part two)

1987

The floor is a recycling bin

green brown clear glass

stabs through the soles

of my Converse

I step light as

six pints allows

and avoid the guy

with no front teeth

who fills up his glass

with everyone's slops

and we're waiting for Hüsker Dü

to scream us into submission

as we pile on each other

rip our eardrums apart

I will never forget you

and it's another night

of energy so high

it bleeds

1988

Bang my head to Gang Green's

alcohol

hold my boyfriend's jacket

fight my way through

concrete spiked hair

board short rags over torn jeans

carrying four beers

splashing on my legs

almost pissing myself

because there's too much

shooting up chucking up

in the toilet hole

and I won't hear anything tomorrow

but this is the life and I want it hard

I don't remember really being aware that girls were in the minority at these gigs. I was having too much fun. I wasn't one for the mosh pit (I blamed it on wearing glasses) but I don't recall thinking I was being excluded for being a girl. There were some girls in the mosh pit – pushing, shoving and slamming – I just wasn't one of them. I liked hanging at the back and taking it all in. I never enjoyed being squashed and preferred my own space to listen and watch. Still do. I don't remember ever seeing any girls on stage at hardcore gigs but I don't think it bothered me. I considered myself a feminist (a working class feminist) and was quite politicised, but I didn't make the connection between the lack of women in the scene and male dominance. That thought came much later. I preferred the company of boys and was considered a tom boy. I didn't think about the pressures to be 'one of the boys' to fit in. I accumulated subcultural capital – I could talk about the bands and I was wearing the right clothes, but looking back, they did treat me differently. In full-tilt naive angry teenage boy mode, 7 Seconds did attempt to address the sexism in the scene in *Not Just Boys' Fun*. At the time I thought this was excellent, 'You feel so fucking threatened/ when they stand out in front/ a stupid, passive piece of meat is all you really want/ but it's not just boys' fun'. When I listen to the song now it makes me cringe a little (something to do with boys speaking for me perhaps?).

Boyfriend's Little Brother's Jacket

No leather for me

already an ALF poster-wielding

vegetarian (freak)

But somehow persuaded (volunteered?)

to paint Pete's jacket

Took it home, steady hand and enamel paint

the Stupids across the top

SST records logo

Black Flag

Minor Threat

At a gig Pete's jacket is spotted

the Stupids reckon it's cool

Who's the artist?

I'm introduced, praised

girls can do something after all?

I can still smell that jacket –

enamel paint and turps couldn't

mask the scent of death

Wonder if Pete still has it?

Still, I felt empowered by the music coming from these (mainly) straight white boys. At odds maybe with my feminism and the diverse friends in my non-hardcore life? The whiteness of the bands (with notable exceptions such as Bad Brains), the homophobia (despite several gay front men in bands) and the overall macho vibe has been acknowledged and problematised in academic work and I'm certainly not defending these elements. But there was something about the music that spoke to me. Something about the anger at governments and institutions, disgust with the greed of the 1980s, the anger at the voicelessness of young people, and the raw emotion of performances that touched a nerve. When I think about it now, I suppose I should've been listening to Discharge and Crass or the political deejays of reggae sound systems, or maybe even Billy Bragg? I missed completely the riot grrl movement of the early 1990s (I was already a mother by then and music took a backseat for a while).

It may seem rather clichéd to suggest that a style of music can change your life, but it did. It made me less apathetic and got me fired up. I wanted to be like Henry Rollins and say 'fuck you!' to authority and stand up to my oppressors. Bad Brains called out those with power, 'You control what I'll be, you control who I see/ and if I let you, you'll control me/ you're the man who owns all the keys to the stores/ you're the man who always wants so much more/ you're the Regulator'. The music was a motivator, an energy starter. I didn't start throwing petrol bombs or manning the barricades, but I did start to take an interest in my workplace and the exploitation there. I took a stand, exposed some of this exploitation via a national newspaper and the conditions for some of workers improved (and cemented my life-long union involvement).

I didn't start my own band to address the gender imbalance, but I became more strident in my political views. The feeling I remember from the gigs and listening to the music as a teenager has remained and I've never lost the hardcore spirit. As naff as it might be for a 45 year old, I still wear Converse, checked shirts (flannelette) and was delighted when skinny black jeans came back in a couple of years ago. Being a hardcore fan made it ok to not be girly and to not be interested in romantic and soppy pop songs and I still get a buzz when I listen to my old records and the words of the songs still resonate.

If I'm on a picket line or joining a march I can still hear Black Flag 'We are tired of your abuse. Try to stop us, it's no use'. Minor Threat's 'Small man. Big Mouth' comes to mind whenever a conservative politician appears on the television (and I'm reading the 'small man' bit as metaphorical rather than a derogatory swipe at men who aren't tall). And I'm pleased to say that I wasn't just influenced by American music – the Subhumans' 'Get to Work on Time' has remained an anthem. This song motivated me to consider life outside of minimum wage and to resist being the slave of an uncaring boss, 'But the choice of ever choosing/ never seemed to cross your mind/ so you go to bed at ten/ you think "never again"/ But you get up in the morning/ and you get to work on time'. Hardcore taught me to stand up for myself and for others (but in a slightly less shouty way).

Back of the Auditorium

Watching the kids smash and slam

sweat flying as hair flicks

beer showers when plastic cups are hurled

Launching themselves off the stage

Someone always climbs the amp

makes that extra leap of faith

Only once do I see the crowd part

hear a thud of body hitting the crusted floor

(he must be a right nob)

I'm at the back

slurping lager

feeling the wave of sound

manic and so loud

it creates a fire in me

but I don't want to flail and punch

I want to think

this is where the music takes me

drums beat away enervation

Whining guitar keeps me focused

I let the sweaty singers shout on my behalf

But I make the words my own

Sarah circa 1987 (doing the washing up – very hardcore!).

It's funny looking back – I wonder if I could've made more of the time (it was so short, most of the bands had disappeared by the late 1980s and I came in quite late). I only have one photograph of me at that time and back then I didn't have the money to buy all the records (gigs weren't so pricey in those days). Most of the music I had was on cassettes, recorded from my boyfriend's large collection. These cassettes were all stolen a few years later when my van got broken into, so there are some bands I've forgotten and songs I can still hear in my head but have never been able to find. I rarely meet other people from this scene, and if I do it's an instant bond. Some of my students know a little about the music and I'm easily distracted from the topic at hand by reminisces and will play Bad Brains' 'I Against I' at every opportunity, 'I said who's gonna tell the youth about the drugs/ about the drugs, mugs, bugs, and the police thugs/ about the rotten stinkin' rackets and the fantasies/ around the nation, around the nations/ oh baby what you gonna do/ I tell you the truth is looking straight at you'.

Now, the music that speaks to me is socially/politically conscious hip hop (especially UK grime). I love the use of language (not so much a forte of the hardcore lyricists) but the anger and passion is still there. Punk is still very much alive, it just has a different accent now.

Postscript

Because I'm an academic (albeit a precariously employed one like so many of us at the moment), I feel I have to include a reading list. Might not be very punk but the artists of the hardcore punk scene certainly taught me a lot about the world.

Bibliography

Attfield, Sarah (2010) 'Hardcore Headfuck: How a Mix Tape of Angry Young Men Spoke to a Working Class Girl' *What's it Worth? Value and Popular Music: Selected Papers from the 2009 IASPM Australia New Zealand Conference*, pp. 2-5.

Blush, Steven (2001) *American Hardcore: A Tribal History*, L.A.: Feral House.

Bock, Jannika (2008) *Riot Grrl: A Feminist Re-interpretation of the Punk Narrative*, Saarbruken: VDM.

Haenfler, Ross (2006) *Straight Edge:Hardcore Punk, Clean Living Youth, and Social Change*, New Jersey: Rutgers University Press.

Hancock, Black Hawk and Lorr, Michael J. (2012) 'More Than Just a Soundtrack: Toward a Technology of the Collective in Hardcore Punk', *Journal of Contemporary Ethnography*, Vol. 42, No.3, pp. 320–346.

Larsen, Al (2013) Fast, cheap and out of control: The graphic symbol in hardcore punk, *Punk & Post Punk*, Vol. 2, No. 1, pp. 91-106.

Leblanc, Lauraine (1999) *Pretty in Punk: Girls' Gender Resistance in a Boys' Subculture*, NY: Rutgers University Press.

McRobbie, Angela (1990) 'Settling Accounts with Subcultures: A Feminist Critique' in Frith, Simon and A. Goodwin (eds) *On Record: Rock, Pop and the Written Word*, London: Routledge.

Rachman, Paul (2006) *American Hardcore: The History of American Punk Rock 1980 – 1986*, Motion Picture, AHC Productions.

Reddington, Helen (2007) *The Lost Women of Rock Music: Female Musicians of the Punk Era*, Aldershot: Ashgate.

Rettman, Tony (2010) *Why Be Something That You're Not: Detroit Hardcore 1979-1985,* CA: Revelation Records.

Reynolds, Simon and Joy Press (1995) *The Sex Revolts: Gender, Rebellion and Rock and Roll*, NY: Serpents Tail.

Tsitsos, William, (1999) 'Rules of Rebellion: Slamdancing, Moshing, and the American Alternative' *Popular Music*, Vol. 18, No. 3 (Oct.), pp. 397-414.

Whitely, Sheila (2000) *Women and Popular Music: Sexuality, Identity, and Subjectivity,* NY: Routledge.

Willis, Susan (1993) 'Hardcore: Subculture American Style' *Critical Inquiry* 19, pp. 365-383.

Discography

Ian McCulloch, Will Sergeant, Les Pattinson, Pete de Freitas, 'The Cutter', *Porcupine*, Korova, 1983.

David Ball, Marc Almond, 'Insecure Me', B-side to 'Torch', Some Bizarre, 1982.

Marc Almond, 'Catch a Fallen Star', *Torment and Toreros*, Some Bizarre, 1983.

Bob Mould, 'I'll Never Forget You', *Zen Arcade*, SST, 1984.

Chuck Stilphen, Chris Doherty, 'Alcohol', *Another Wasted Night*, Taang! Records, 1986.

Kevin Seconds, 'Not Just Boys' Fun', *The Crew*, BYO, 1984.

Bad Brains, 'The Regulator', *Bad Brains*, ROIR, 1982.

Greg Ginn, 'Rise Above', *Damaged*, SST Records, 1981.

Ian MacKaye, 'Small Man, Big Mouth', *Minor Threat*, Dischord, 1984.

Subhumans 'Get to Work on Time', *Worlds Apart*, Bluurg, 1985.

Paul Hudson, Darryl Jenifer, Gary Miller, 'I Against I', *I Against I*, SST, 1986.

Crass/UK Subs Gig Poster by Persons Unknown

You Can Live Forever In Paradise On Earth *Ted Curtis*

You live in the most beautiful city in the world and for the past two years you have been part of an underground cult. It's the cult with no name, but recently the music press has begun referring to it as *anarcho punk,* and although this has initially given you a vague kind of thrill, this minor recognition for something you usually have to explain to people at length, deep inside you don't desire that recognition, you don't want mainstream society to have any kind of claim to ownership over this thing that you dropped out of school for, although you spent most of your time there staring out of windows and praying for the ring of the bell before your name was called, somehow you believed that now you had found the answer, the solution to *the war in your head*, so you dropped out, and you joined the cult with no name, where you were never really welcome.

You walk into the *Hat & Feather* pub on Walcot street, renowned in local hippie lore throughout the 1970s and 1980s. It's a Sunday night, it's cold, you have no money and you spend most of your time walking the streets, looking for familiar faces that aren't there, waiting for something to happen, wanting for something to happen. Afraid to go back to the freezing squat where you live alone, with neither electricity nor running water, where night after night you sit by candlelight, writing angry lyrics to uncomposed punk songs that nobody will hear. Strumming along in vain on an electric guitar that will never be plugged into a power source, the plastic nut chipped at one end where you dropped it in the road when you were drunk, the electric guitar that will never be able to accommodate a top e string, that your mother signed the hire purchase forms for in Duck Son & Pinker because you were not yet eighteen, and you walk into the *Hat & Feather* pub on Walcot street. It is warm and not too crowded, and you like that it is not too crowded because already you do not like to be around people very much, but in one corner that is fortuitously the corner nearest to you, as you walk through the door, sitting on a table in the corner with his cherry reds, that is what he calls his bruised and battered old Doctor Marten boots with mismatched laces, his cherry reds, sitting on a table with his cherry reds on a rickety old chair, rocking it back and forth, is Chris Palmer. And Chris Palmer has a pint of lager and he is singing along to something on the jukebox, it's *the jam*, it's *tales from the riverbank*, he throws his head back and he sings, exposing his rotting teeth, *now life is so critical, life is too cynical, we lose our innocence we lose our very souuul, ahh...* and sitting on another rickety chair is Dawn Willis, and as you walk over she looks up, and she sees you and smiles, and Chris Palmer looks across and he sees you and through those blackened teeth, he smiles too.

You say hello and you begin chatting but there are no handshakes, you never shake hands with anyone, shaking hands seems too businesslike, it seems too much like the world of commerce, too much like the world of capitalism that you are attempting to escape from, the world of capitalism that you want to destroy, although you do not have any kind of a program for this, you do not have any kind of a program for anything, because having a program would mean selling out, it would mean being organized, it would mean being too much like *them*. That's how it is, it's *us and them*. So instead of shaking hands you chat away about the song and about *the jam*, you chat away about how you saw them at Bath Pavilion and at the Royal Bath & West Showground, and then mid-sentence Chris Palmer leans into your ear and he whispers above the noise, *buy us a pint Ted*, and you tell him that you can't, because you have no money, and Chris Palmer hands his pint to you and you drain half of it and you hand the almost empty glass back to him, and he polishes it off and he wipes the last of it from his lips with the back of his hand, he slams the glass down hard onto the rickety old table, which makes Dawn Willis wince, and Chris Palmer steps back and reaches into his jeans pocket and he says to you, *I'll buy you a pint Ted, you're a good man, I saw me old dear earlier and she gave me a fiver*, and he walks two steps over and he leans on the bar, and he calls out for service, and he gets you a pint and he gets himself a pint, and he gets Dawn Willis a half of mild, because that's what she likes, and then his money is gone too, and you are all very happy. And as *tales from the riverbank* segues seamlessly into *a town called malice*, you begin to talk about the old days, and all the bands that you saw, although there are not all that many old days, not yet, because you are nineteen and he is twenty, you have only known each other for a couple of years. After having known each other for six months you made a suicide pact together, not because you were depressed, although you are, even if you do not know this yet, even if you will not know this for quite a few years yet, no, you made a suicide pact because neither of you ever want to be twenty-one. The age at which most people, apparently, sell out.

And you talk about the old days and you talk about *the jam* because Chris Palmer was not always an anarcho punk, Chris Palmer was once a mod, he was once the king of the mods, he was once the king of the jam boys in the most beautiful city in the world. But you were never a mod because you were too fat, even though you had the desert boots, and the stripey boating blazer, bought on HP, from your mother's Littlewoods catalogue, 38 weeks at 75 pence. And you wear them sometimes still, in combination, with your raggedy black jeans, held together with safety pins, and a *fuck authority* patch, and your crazy colour shocking pink Mohawk, the sides badly shaved, all scabby and spotty. And one time Chris Palmer is holding forth, standing in front of a bricked up fireplace in a candlelit room, at #4 Railway Place, and he calls you *my mate Fred Dread with the scabby head*, and he tells you that he likes you, he tells you that he loves you, but that bits of you just don't seem to fit together, referring to the desert boots, and the stripey blazer, and the shocking pink Mohawk, with the sides badly shaved. And still you share a love of *the jam,* and of *the lambrettas* and *Billy Bragg* with Chris Palmer, and this sets you apart from the other members of the cult, and in later years you will come to realize that all of this was subconscious, all of this ingratiating yourself into the smallest culty little pop music tribe that you could find, and then setting yourself apart from most of the other members of that tribe, it was all subconscious, it sprang from a longing to be utterly alone, to be completely isolated, even within the confines of an invisible subgroup, most of the members of which would very soon either sell out or die. But Chris Palmer comes from a more deprived social background than you, even though you are both working class, he comes from an estate called Whiteway on the south side, his parents divorced, his father a moribund alcoholic. Whiteway is the largest council estate in the most beautiful city in the world, apart from Snowhill on the east side where his moribund alcoholic father now lives. And because Chris Palmer comes from Whiteway, and because he grew up with divorced parents and in relative poverty, because he went to Culverhay, the hardest school in the most beautiful city in the world, at the bottom of Rush Hill, which is handy for Whiteway, and which is now gone, because of all this he discovered glue sniffing in his early teens, and he found glue sniffing to be really quite liberating, he found it to be a beautiful experience, that it made the world go away, and he found that it really did make quiet *the war in his head*. But there are down sides to glue sniffing for a well dressed mod, and one summer night after he had gone bagging it with some friends from Culverhay and from Whiteway, in the woods near Englishcombe village, where your parents were married, he had blacked out. Like you do, with the glue sniffing, with the solvent abuse. And after he blacked out his friends had left him for dead, and he woke up alone with the worst headache of his life, and to find that his £200 tonic suit had all of these dead leaves stuck fast to it, and his best paisley shirt too, and his face, and that the suit and the shirt were ruined. And so he resolved not to stop glue sniffing, which he found to be such a liberating experience, which he found had really quieted *the war in his head*. No, he resolved instead to stop being a mod, and instead to become an anarchist punk, because he knew about music, he knew about subcultures, and he knew that the anarchist punks dressed all in black rags and all in black rage, and that these rags and this rage would hardly show up a few dead leaves and ingrained Evo-Stik stains. But perversely of course, as soon as he had ingratiated himself into the subcultural world of anarchist punk, he found it so exciting, he found it to be so invigorating, all of the freer than free festivals and all of the hitch hiking up and down the country to gigs in scout huts and rundown community centres, and to wildcat political demonstrations, never quite knowing just where he would end up, he found all of that to be so exciting and liberating that the desire for solvent abuse soon left him, and he became an acid punk, *acid punks and hardcore hippies*, and now here you stand together, with Dawn Willis sitting, in the *Hat & Feather* pub on Walcot Street. And Chris Palmer turns away from the bar, he puts his back to the bar, and he reaches into the arse pocket of his raggedy black jeans, and pulls something out and unfolds it, and discreetly he shakes some amphetamine sulphate, first into his pint, and then into yours, and soon you are talking, ten to the dozen, about the old days, about *the jam* and *the lambrettas* and *Billy Bragg*. And then a new song comes onto the jukebox, and it is *99 red balloons* by *nena*, and you talk ten to the dozen about the lyrics to the song, because you both find it so hard to believe, with your siege mentality, that anything in the mainstream could possibly be referring to a nuclear war. And this is the last drink that you will ever have with Chris Palmer, the former king of the mods, the anarchist punk.

You first met Chris Palmer when you were in a band in the sixth form at school, a band called *the end*. You did rock and roll covers, together with Marcus Hulme and Neil Palmer and Stephen Vincent, Marcus Hulme who was a classically trained double bass player and a Beatles fanatic, so you did rock and roll covers from the glory days of the Beatles, from *before they went all funny* as your mother would say, as well as a few three chord compositions that Marcus Hulme and Neil Palmer had penned themselves. Marcus Hulme had singled you out at school as a loner, an interesting misfit, an angry loser, somebody like him, and he had heard you wrote punk lyrics, that you were telling people you were going to get a band together, called *toxic vomit*, but that you had never got as far as taking any concrete steps to form this band. And so he approached you, and he offered you *the end* as your backing band, and you agreed. But before you had a chance to arrange a practice, the lead guitarist of *the end* left to pursue a career at the Ministry of Defence, and so you were reined in as the new lead guitarist, and Marcus Hulme bought you a guitar, he taught you the basics, he lent you his *guitar case chord book*, and you practiced together, mostly at *dizzy miss lizzie* by the Beatles and *smoke on the water* by *deep purple*, but you only did one gig, at the *ring o bells* in Widcombe. And Chris Palmer saw you there, and a couple of weeks later, as you were walking home from practice, across the Bear Flat, Chris Palmer, pissed out of his head, calls out to you from the other side of the road, and he begins crossing the road and running towards you. And you and Marcus Hulme looks at each other, not saying a word, but your faces saying, do we run do we run? But as you are both pinhead geeks who didn't go to the hardest school, you do not run, you merely walk faster, and Chris Palmer catches up with you, and you stop walking, and Chris Palmer puts his hand onto Marcus Hulme's shoulder, then he braces his knees, trying to get back his breath, he puts one finger on one nostril, expels snot through the other, onto the pavement, so that it doesn't get onto his jolly mod clothes. And he stands up straight again, and Marcus Hulme says to him, shaking and stammering, *y-y-yes, h-h-hello?*

And Chris Palmer explains, still catching his breath, that he saw you, at *the ring o bells* in Widcombe the weekend before, and he tells you *you were shit*, he tells you that *you were really fucking crap*, and you look at Chris Palmer, Chris Palmer is staring, his eyelids not blinking, right at you and through you. And as you look at Chris Palmer he repeats the lines to you, *you were shit mate, you were fucking crap, you really were*, but then he sees your expression, slightly crestfallen and slightly afraid, and he adds an addendum, he looks you in the eye, he squints very slightly, and he says, *but you had fucking bollocks, you had fucking balls, you're not going to give up are you, never give up mate, never fucking give up*. And he slaps you on the shoulder, and he turns to Marcus Hulme, says the same thing to him, he says *never give up mate, never fucking give up*. Then he puts out his hand, and he shakes your hand, and he shakes Marcus Hulme's hand, and then he is gone. And you stand for a moment, you and Marcus Hulme, on the Bear Flat, and Marcus Hulme says to you, still shaking still stammering, *w-w-wow, that was really f-f-frightening, I think I need a cup of tea.*

And the next time you meet, you and Chris Palmer, it is at #4 Railway Place, an enormous squat, sandwiched between the railway station and the GPO sorting office. You have brought him your fanzine, it is hand done in biro, but there is nobody in, Railway Place is a skeleton, a hulking gothic ruin, its front windows smashed, the electricity disconnected. And you stand there for a while, in the December cold, and along comes a crusty, before there were crusties, with his curly black hair all matted in dreadlocks, before it was fashionable for white men to have dreadlocks. And he says *alright mate, have you got a key?* thinking that you might live there too. And you say to him *no mate, sorry mate, I don't have a key*, and he raises his eyebrows, and says to you conspiratorially, *well now, it looks like we're going to have to break in then doesn't it?* And he clambers up a drainpipe, and he gets into #4 Railway Place, through a tiny bathroom window, but he leaves you standing, there on the pavement, in the December cold, he doesn't come down the stairs to let you in. And you stand there waiting, thinking maybe he's forgotten me, maybe he needed a dump or something, and about ten minutes later Chris Palmer comes along, shambling around the corner, he isn't a mod anymore, he wears a raggedy greatcoat, drainpipe jeans fixed with safety pins and black bandages, he wears his cherry reds, one side of his head shaved, the other done up in soapy red spikes, and he says *oh hello there*. He's been out drinking with his dad, the alcoholic John Palmer, and he bangs on the door, for a further three minutes, calling out *let us in let us in*, and eventually the crusty comes to the door, and he lets you both in, and he says to you, *oh hello again mate, I didn't know that you wanted to come in, you didn't say.*

And you go inside with Chris Palmer, you go up to his room, where by the light of a moribund candle, you show him your fanzine, and again he says, *this is shit Ted, this is fucking crap, it really is.* And he asks you if you have any money, and you tell him that you do, you tell him that you have about a pound, from your paper round, and he says, *buy us a cup of tea then*, and so you go with him the bus station café, where the tea is cheap, and you sit there in the warm, both of you nursing your black tea, because of course you are vegans, because it is extreme, and it's just before closing, just before kicking out time, and you natter and chatter, about bands and revolution, and as they are kicking you out, as the café is closing, he asks you where you live, and you tell him *Odd Down, at the house of my parents*, and he tells you should squat, he says *you should rebel*, he says you should break out of your conformity, *because revolution begins at home,* he tells you.

And after that there are many squats, and many anarchist punk gigs, in a short space of time, and one time you are at a festival, you and Chris Palmer, it's the last Stonehenge festival, on midsummer's night, in the June of 1984. You have dropped acid together, you and Chris Palmer, *red hearts £1:50*, the sort that the *hardcore hippies* call *disco acid*, they don't consider it powerful, not like it was in the sixties. And you are cresting on the acid, you are peaking on the acid, because it seems very powerful, and it seems very peaceful, in this field at this festival, on midsummer's day. And as you lie there on your fronts, your boots off, in a half deserted field, in front of a stage, where other people in sleeping bags are waiting for the sunrise, and are waiting for *hawkwind* to perform their *space ritual*, the sun comes up, cresting the horizon, peaking over Amesbury. And Chris Palmer looks at you, and Chris Palmer says to you, *there it is, the light of the world.* And at first it is slow, just the topside of a disc of burning red fire, of hydrogen and helium, this four and a half billion year old never-ending reaction, like an infinite Hiroshima, but beautiful so beautiful, and then it gets faster, and it changes its colours, and a rainbow comes out of it, and it does a double-dip, skips across the horizon, and you follow it with your eyeballs, the ghosting of the burning red disc playing games on your retinae, and then it skips back again, back into the sun. And both of you aghast, both of you speechless, Chris Palmer looks at you again, as if to say, *did you see it did you see it*, and you nod and you smile, and then he says something else, he says *did you ever think that there might be something more to it than this... life?* But you don't quite hear him, you are trying to blink away the ghosts in your eyes, the rainbows and red splotches, of the nuclear reaction, 93 million miles away, this infinite Hiroshima. So you say to him *what, Chris?* and then he changes tack, he asks you if you ever met Sean Crooks, and you say that no you didn't, you say that you've heard of him, you say *didn't he used to know crass or something?* And under his breath you think you hear him say, *and the lamb shall lay down with the lion,* and you wonder what he's seen, and you ask him what he said, but he doesn't seem to hear you, and it all seems so perfect, it all seems so complete, lying here in this field, that you don't want to push it. And then there is a noise, a hum of sub-feedback, and you look to the stage, and *hawkwind* are there, *hawkwind* are tuning up, to perform their *space ritual*, and then they are off, into *silver machine*, and before you know it you are both asleep.

And eventually you find yourself back at the house of your parents, and Chris Palmer has moved back in with his mother, because neither of you seem able to get along with other people, even in this tiny subculture with no rules, and where the cry is always *anarchy!* And you don't see each other for a couple of weeks, but you have heard all the rumours, you have heard all the gossip, because this scene thrives on rumours, this scene thrives on gossip. Because it is only a microcosm, dependent on the macrocosm of the society it despises. And the rumours are saying that Chris Palmer has become a Jehovah's Witness, that he has given himself over to Jesus, like Sean Crooks before him, like Sean Crooks whom you have never met, but who was once friends with *Crass*. And you don't believe the rumours, you think that they are bullshit, because you believe all the bullshit, all the other bullshit, about thinking for yourself, about being open-minded, and so you don't believe the rumours.

And so one day you call him, and his mother picks up the phone, and Chris Palmer comes to the phone and he speaks to you. And for a while it is normal, just normal conversation, about who you have and haven't seen, and the gigs you haven't been to, because they're getting quite boring. About *the jam* and *crass* and the *sex pistols* and the *smartpils*, and all of the things, that you used to get up to, back in the day. And you are saying something, and he stops you short, and you ask what's the matter, and he says: *you swore at me, please don't swear at me Jer*. And you notice for the first time, that all the way through this telephone conversation, he has been calling you *Jer*. Not *Ted*, but *Jer*. Only your mother calls you *Jer*. And you ask him why he is calling you *Jer*, not *Ted* but *Jer*, because only your mother calls you *Jer*, and he tells you he is calling you *Jer* because your name is *Jeremy*, your name is not *Ted*, your name is *Jeremy*, it's the name your parents chose for you, and he tells you that you should honour your mother and father. He tells you it says in the bible that you should honour your mother and your father. And you ask him *what the fucking problem with swearing is*, and he tells you again *please don't swear at me Jer*, and you say to him *OK OK, what is your problem with swearing* Christopher? *It's just language. It's only words*, you say. And he tells you, *because all sin comes form the same place Jer*. And you realize that the rumours are true, that the gossip isn't hearsay, but still you press on, with the conversation, because you were close with him once, and not so long ago, you saw the world in the same way, you dropped acid together, and you wondered at the wonder, and so you wonder you wonder, if there might be something in it. Because the way that the world sees Jehovah's Witnesses is not all that different from the way the world sees anarchist punks, and anyway, something in you rather likes the idea of an apocalypse cult. Because anarchist punk is an apocalypse cult too. All of the songs that you sing along and dance to seem to be about nuclear war, *they've got a bomb, the possibility of life's destruction, cruise missiles have arrived, contaminational power*. And so you agree to meet him, at his new place, which he shares with Dawn Palmer, because now they are married, although you were not invited. And together you study the two sacred books of the Jehovah's Witnesses, designed for unbelievers, with plenty of pictures, those bad water colours, one is red one is blue. The blue one disproves evolution and is called, *life - how did it get here?* and the red one is called, *you can live forever in paradise on earth*. And when they speak of their new beliefs, Dawn and Chris Palmer, they refer to it as *the truth*, they say *does he know the truth yet?* Like Margaret Thatcher, saying *is he one of us?* And he tells you why they don't celebrate Christmas, because Christmas is a lie, because it says in the bible that the shepherds were out tending their flocks, but in depths of winter it would have been too cold for them to do that. And you swallow this whole, not thinking that maybe, in the middle east in December, things might have been warmer than they are here in England, in the 20th Century. And he tells you Jehovah's Witnesses do not celebrate birthdays either, and you ask him why this is, and he tells you that it's because birthdays are egotistical, because celebrating your own birthday is narcissistic, he tells you that you should love god and not yourself, because loving god *is* loving yourself, because *without god we are nothing*, without god we are *doomed to hell, without god we would not exist at all*. And you say to him you don't mind that, because nobody ever remembers your birthday anyway, and you ask him if he knows when your birthday is, and he looks at you sideways. And he turns the page of the red book, and over the page of the red book is an awful watercolour of two white people, and their two white children, lying down in a field, with a lion and a lamb. And they're watching the sun rise, and the caption says *what is life really all about?* And he turns and he says to you, *don't you remember that, Jer? Don't you remember lying in a field at Stonehenge or Stoney Cross, or some other scabby festival, some other illegal festival, all of us off our heads on dangerous mind-bending drugs, and thinking, what's it all about? What is life all about? Isn't that what we were always looking for? All of us lost children? All of us poor lost god's children? Well, this is it Jer, this is it!*

And there's other stuff too, like his explanation that the war in heaven, where Lucifer the rebellious angel staged an attempted coup against god, because he resented god's power, god's unelected power, he resented god's authority, and you think of that patch, that you used to wear, that said *fuck authority*. And Lucifer thought that maybe somebody else should get to have a go, and that he might just be that somebody else. And there was a war in heaven, and Lucifer loses, and Lucifer and the other angels he had managed to rally round him, to rally to his cause, of *fuck authority*, they lose the war in heaven, because god is all-powerful. And god casts out Lucifer, and his rebellious angels, he casts them out of heaven, and they fall to the earth. And the angels become demons, and Lucifer remains Lucifer, except now he's called Satan, and the earth is hell. And Chris Palmer explains to you that all of this happened during the great war, that all of this was the reason for the great war, the war of 1914-1918, that hell on earth, he tells you that *it all makes sense Jer. Don't you see?* And you're a little unsure of this, because you think that god and heaven probably exist outside of time, because time is a human construct, used to measure the days and rates of decay, and the heartbeats between sunrises. And you tell Chris Palmer this, and he says that the demons are trying to confuse you. And he explains it all further, saying this was when the rot set in, this was when everything else began to go wrong, this was when the moral bankruptcy and decay began to manifest themselves, everything since 1918: disobedience to parents, drug abuse, pop music, dating. And you think about asking if he's read the Old Testament, the genocides, the stonings, the misogyny, the slavery, the plagues, the flood, but you think better of it. Because you know that he will say that all of these things were god's will. And you remember your suicide pact, and that now Chris Palmer thinks that he is going to *live forever in paradise on earth*. But at once you feel part of it, this apocalypse cult, where nobody is telling you what clothes to wear or what food to eat. You feel you are in it already, this hankering for belonging, and for simple explanations to impossible questions.

And all of the people you speak to afterwards, all the other anarchist punks, about the Jehovah's witnesses, they all say to you, *it's a cult Ted, it's a cult*. And one is appalled when you tell him, in all seriousness, in the *Hat & Feather*, that you think that's it's probably the best religion. *That's shit Ted* he says, *that's such shit, what about Buddhism?*, but you don't know about Buddhism. And all of this time your punk life, with the glue and speed and cider crazed nights at the Longacre Hall, with the *smartpils* and *antisect* and the *hippy slags*, in Snowhill, where Chris Palmer's moribund alcoholic father John lives, is going on in tandem, with the Bible study sessions, and the Friday night visits to their church in Walcot, the *Kingdom Hall*, which is only a stone's throw from Snowhill, and the Longacre Hall. And your mum speaks to you about it, she's seen the copies of *the watchtower* and *awake!* lying around in your bedroom, replacing the gig flyers and the BUAV flyers, and she says to you, *I don't like those people, they twist things*. Listen to your mother. Disobedience to parents.

And Chris had been a cartoonist, a talented and vitriolic artist. And he had drawn one cartoon, a cartoon of himself, with the top of his head flipped open, a roll-up hanging from one side of his mouth, his eyes glazed, his brain exposed. And with a businessman, a priest and a military general, all sucking out his brains through drinking straws. And someone has kept hold of this cartoon, he has put it in his fanzine, which is called *die, you fucker!* And underneath it he has scrawled, *what a waste of talent Chris, your mind's been well fucked with now.*

But in the end you abandon it, this apocalypse cult, with its simple explanations to impossible questions, the Jehovah's Witnesses, although you never quite were one. And you move to Swindon, for what you think might be love, but above all to be running, to always be running. But you think of it often, the acid at Stonehenge, and that last drink with Chris Palmer, in the *Hat & Feather*, and that speed in your pint, and *Billy Bragg* and *the jam*, and *99 red balloons*. And one time in Swindon the Jehovah's Witnesses come to your door, you have a bag on your head, you are dyeing your hair, you are dyeing it purple, and you ask them about the red book and the blue book, and they are taken aback, that you know all their secrets, perhaps they think you are a demon, and in the end you just tell them, no thank you, I think I'm in a cult already, one cult is enough for anybody, and they leave.

Because anarchist punk has its unwritten rules: the rigid uniform of the all-black clothes, the absolute conformity of the pacifism, the veganism. It is all about anarchy, and there are no rules, instead an unwritten code of conformity: all of those invisible rules you must adhere to, just to be accepted. It's just another cult, one that thinks it's so different, as every cult must, or else no-one would join. And you wear it in your heart, and you write it on your clothes. It's a cult. It's a cult. It's a cult.

Sothira Pheng – Crucifix – by Jacky Smith

Biographies

Alastair Gordon

Alastair 'Gords' Gordon likes all things DiY punk rock and always knew he was out of step with the world. He's been involved in the punk scene for longer than he'd like to remember. He became a 'punkademic' via an early, total rejection of formal schooling and its traditional teaching methods. He completed a doctorate on Authenticity and DiY punk under the supervision of Professor Mike Pickering (Loughborough University). Gords informs his academic research through playing in bands and remains active in the UK and international DiY punk scenes. He currently vents anger at the world singing, touring and recording with the band Geriatric Unit and playing bass in Endless Grinning Skulls. He is currently a senior lecturer in Media and Communication and De Montfort University, Leicester. He also co runs the Punk Scholar Network with Mike Dines, Pete Dale, Russ Bestley & Matt Worley. Gords fucking hates Tories of all political
colours.

Alistair Livingston

After seeing the Rezillos play in his Scottish home town in the summer of 77, Alistair Livingston cut his hair and shaved off his beard. In 79 he started work in a condom factory in London and soon discovered Kill Your Pet Puppy fanzine and anarchist inspired punk. In 84/5 he managed the Mob's All the Madmen record company. He married Pinki a punk who became a Greenham woman. After Pinki died he moved back to Scotland in 1997. In 2005 he started green Galloway blog which was meant to be about windmills and psychedelic dreams but is now mainly about punk as a counterculture. http://greengalloway.blogspot.co.uk/

Alistair's contribution to Tales from the Punk side was written for a conference on 'Contemporary Anarchism in Theory and Practice'. Unlike most anarcho-punks, Alistair had become a self-confessed anarchist before punk discovered anarchy in 1976. Most accounts of anarcho-punk focus on its emergence as a musical style out of punk. But the intersection with punk also influenced anarchism as a culture of resistance. Written for an anarchist audience, Alistair's account of anarcho-punk therefore focuses on the politics not the music and continues the story on through opposition to the Poll Tax in 1990 to the present and his involvement with the Radical Independence Campaign in Scotland.

Amanda Bigler

Amanda Bigler received her BA in English Literature with a Creative Writing emphasis from the University of Kansas in the United States. In 2010 she was awarded the University of Kansas' Creative Writing award for her short work, "Tightrope." She then completed her MA in Literature with a negotiated pathway from Loughborough University in 2013. Currently, she is a postgraduate research student at Loughborough University. Amanda's research focuses on contemporary literature, humanist American and British literature, and technology's influence on current literature in a post-postmodern era. Amongst her publications are: "Unorganis(z)ed Chaos" (You Is for University), "On the River's Edge" (The StoryGraph, thestorygraph.com), "Patriots, Lobsters, and Nudity: Exploring Situational Irony in Contemporary American Humorist Literature" (New Writing: The International Journal for the Practice and Theory of Creative Writing), and "Cloven" (Goldsmiths Literature Seminar (GLITS) e-journal of criticism).

Francis Stewart

Francis Stewart grew up in Northern Ireland and discovered punk in her early teens (early 90s) through the late, great John Peel, the not late but equally great Terri Hooley and the fantastic pirate radio stations that came up Belfast loch. Despite finding punk the perfect soundtrack to the environment she left in the late 90s to attend university and "be a grown up". That didn't work out so well so instead she turned her love of punk into a doctoral thesis and now pretends to be a grown up by playing punk rock and talking about it (vaguely intelligently on a good day) at Stirling University while contributing to numerous zines on and offline.

The Outcasts (named after one of the most important but overshadowed Northern Irish punk bands of The Troubles) is a reflection of an early introduction to punk at a time when nothing made sense, everything was kicking off and blowing up and yet the angry outcasts were able to use their music to create their own community. It also reflects on punk's propensity to look back at itself through rose-tinted glasses (or maybe that should be beer googles) and be highly selective with its back story.

Greg Bull

Greg Bull heard the Sex Pistols as a 12 year old and liked the noise they made. He liked their energy. He liked their attitude. And he liked their dress-sense and their rejection of authority. He didn't really know or understand this at the time as he just felt these things without understanding them. But he didn't become a punk then.

Later in the early 1980s Greg met up with like-minded individuals who turned him on to "Black and White" bands such as Crass, and he met and went to see Antisect quite a few times as well. He listened to a wide-range of music though and avoided proper "work" until the mid 1990s. He is writing things down now from his memory of those times. And working on co-editing a few books on punk whilst his own work Perdam Babylonis Nomen is going to press Summer 2014

Helen Reddington

While attending Brighton Art College in 1976 I became waylaid by punk. After touring for seven years I burned out and started working on estates in South London as a song writing facilitator, before joining the new Commercial Music BA at the University of Westminster as a lecturer.
That is where I completed a PhD which became my book *The Lost Women of Rock Music: female musicians of the punk era* (2007 Ashgate/1012 Equinox).

http://www.equinoxpub.com/equinox/books/showbook.asp?bkid=489

I also contributed chapters to *The Post Subcultures Reader* and *Music, Power and Politics*. I am now based at the University of East London where I lecture in Songwriting and Production. I am currently researching other punk-related subjects and also female producers and engineers in the UK, as well as performing/recording solo under the name Helen McCookerybook; this year I toured the UK supporting my partner's band, Martin Stephenson and The Daintees, and I have just released an album of skiffle songs which can be found here

https://helenmccookerybook.bandcamp.com/album/anarchy-skiffle

I have recently been working with Gina Birch of The Raincoats. I am also an illustrator and contributed work to *Punkademics* and *Let's Start a Pussy Riot*; I illustrated the cover of the *We're All In This Together* CD released by The Morning Star Newspaper and I'm just about to start the Guerilla Drawfare project, which will involve targeting recording studios with feminist comic stories and other seditious publications.

Facebook artist page https://www.facebook.com/pages/Helen-McCookerybook/346530963905?ref=hl

My blog can be found at mccookerybook.blogspot.co.uk

Illustrations at mccookerybook.tumblr.com

Isabel Flores

"Always in search for the ideal world, but there is no such..." the psychologist told Isabel one day and it all made sense. It was not acceptance but the perfect explanation of her doings. It all started with Dracula at age 12 giving way to Goth Music in high-school, one of the many spawns of Punk yet the eeriest, walking every Saturday for 4 years to the Chopo Rock Street Market until becoming a singer herself of a very garage punk band while teaching English at a public high-school ever trying to change the minds. Woman, Goth, contester, ever questioning everything and everyone, herself included, Isabel became a Cybernetician and a Museologist, both professions paradoxically have complemented themselves in the pursue of the dream, to let people know that music can actually change the world, and for that she makes use of memory. Working on an oral history of Riot Grrrls in México, a digital library on Mexican and South American Rock, and as researcher on Street Art. Might not change the world but might make good noise to reach the ideal.

(A brief description of the work submitted.)

Oral History of Marcos Suárez, "El Marilyn", alternative medicien practicioner, visual and fashion artist but above all Punk to his backbone in México. "Juzga tu persona" (Judge your own person) was the first phrase he coined in a T-shirt and one of the many actions he is always remembered.

At the Chopo Rock Street Market these days is quite difficult to bump into Marcos Suarez a.k.a. "El Marilyn", one of the very first punks in Mexico City. With some luck and thanks to "La Flans", I had the honor to record and listen to his story. Through Memory, promises are kept and history stops being a fabrication to become action.

Justine Butler

Justine grew up in the suburbs just outside London in the 70's. She says it was great time and place to be a teenage punk. She moved to Bristol in the early 80's, signed on the dole and lived in a series of squats for nearly a decade. Drumming in all-girl punk band and living through the lives and deaths of those around her, Justine gained a valuable insight into what is now called the punk subculture.

Disgustin' Justin - the story of a teenage punk

Justine's story focuses on what it was like to be young in the 70's, the Winter of Discontent, Thatcher's electoral victory, The Falklands War and the Miner's Strikes... Rebellion in the air and life was an adventure that we'll never experience again in the same way. No one had mobile phones, no Facebook, no internet even! Most people were in a band at some point or other and mucking about and having a laugh was a priority! Heroin reared it's ugly head and took a good few friends away. Eventually those that survived grew up a bit but we keep the spirit of punk very close by...

Laura Way

Laura currently teaches anthropology/sociology in FE in order to fund her part-time punk PhD. The former mostly involves spreading a love of Karl Marx's facial hair and searching for the ultimate sociological meme.

Lucy Robinson

Lucy Robinson is Senior Lecturer in Modern British History at the University of Sussex. Her first monograph 'Gay Men and the Left in Post-war Britain: How the personal got political' was published by MUP in 2007. Since then she has published on Falklands veterans' experiences of trauma, politics and pop music, and the history of radical teaching in universities. As well as academic publications, Lucy regularly appears in the media and collaborates with various popular cultural practitioners from songwriters, to documentary makers, and burlesque dancers. She jointly coordinates two projects; The Subcultures Network and the open access digital resource 'Observing the 80s'. She is now writing a book on meanings of time, politics and popular culture in the 1980s. She loves Elvis.

Martin Cooper

Martin Cooper is also known as Martin Fish, foul-mouthed fat man of the world's only scatological punk rock/music hall crossover act, The Fish Brothers. After scratching around squats and Second World War bunkers in the "pathetically named" Salad From Atlantis, supporting fine bands such as the Astronauts, Blyth Power and Citizen Fish (no relation), the soon-to-be fat one decided to ditch the cod politics and write the songs that make the young girls sick. The Fish Brothers are currently working on a new album, provisionally entitled Go Fourth And Multiply, a sure-fire blockbuster that will be fit to follow the beautifully manicured Sgt Shitter's Lonely Club Foot Band; Follow Thru; Number Two; and The Difficult Turd Album (spot the theme running through it?). El Fat Custard also had a short story published in Gobbing, Pogoing and Gratuitous Bad Language!: An Anthology of Punk Short Stories (Spare Change Books) and is co-author of the cult (sic) novel Seaton Point. www.thefishbrothers.com and Faceache

Rebecca Binns

Rebecca Binns is about to start a PHD at UAL on Gee Vaucher's graphics for various outlets including Crass. She also writes for Source photography magazine and contributes articles on art, architecture, squatting and homelessness on a freelance basis to several other publications. In the 80s, Rebecca attempted to resuscitate 70s punk via the usual teenage routes of locking herself in her bedroom with a stack of vinyl and forming a band. This led to her discovery of an emerging scene full of similarly disgruntled individuals, intent on creating something alternative. Rebecca found herself pushed into living out her punkish rebellion when she ended up homeless at the age of seventeen.

This contribution recounts Rebecca's experiences living within a subterranean world of punk-squatters in London in the late 80s. To try to recapture the excitement and raw energy, her memories, refracted through age, experience and the formalised language of academia are interspersed with diary entries, photographs, letters and gig tickets from the time. Central to Rebecca's interest is an exploration of whether punk identity was integral to people's decision to squat, or something that was adopted through squatting. Her other focus is on what motivated people to squat, and how this experience provided invaluable freedom alongside new traps.

She can be contacted via her linkedin account at:

https://www.linkedin.com/profile/view?id=82338094&trk=nav_responsive_tab_profile

Robert Dellar

Robert Dellar is author of *Splitting in Two: Mad Pride and Punk Rock Oblivion* (Unkant, 2014), editor of the short story collection *Gobbing, Pogoing & Gratuitous Bad Language* (1996), co-editor of the anthology *Mad Pride: A Celebration of Mad Culture* (2000) and co-author of the novel *Seaton Point* (1998). Starting with the punk fanzine *Breach of the Peace*, he has published underground magazines prolifically since 1980, most recently *Southwark Mental Health News*. He works in the mental health field and lives in South London. He can be contacted C/O SAMH, Cambridge House, 1 Addington Square, London SE5 0HF.

Crusty is one of a series of "rock 'n' roll" short stories originally written during the 1990s but never published in paperback form. A version of it appeared in Andy Martin's magazine *Smile*, but the typeface was too small for it to be legible. There's no point to this story.

Sarah Attfield

Sarah Attfield is originally from London, but now lives in Australia where she works as an academic. Her work focuses on popular culture and social class and she is interested in the ways in which working class people are represented in pop culture and how working class people produce pop culture. This is due to her own working class background. She also writes and publishes poetry (her creative work deals with working class experience). She still listens to her hardcore punk records when no one else is home.

Ted Curtis

Ted Curtis had a somewhat sheltered working class childhood, but in 1983 he saw Crass and ran away with the anarchist punk circus. He thought they meant every word they said. He recently finished a radio play on the jam, the miners strike and the IRA, and is working on a collection of short stories about Swindon in the 1980s. Random samples of new work can be found at http://antsy-pantsy.blogspot.com/ During the nineties he had some success in the small press, but decided to concentrate on his drinking instead. He was very good at it too. Now he's back.

You can live forever is about youth, friendship, naivety, corruption, and the simple solutions to complex problems that all cults offer. Chris Palmer was a complex man, but a true individual, and although he donned the uniform of anarcho, he remained a free thinker right up to his seduction by the Jehovah's Witnesses. This forms part of a narrative challenging the modern bourgeois perception that the 1980s anarcho scene was a garden of eden, where the lamb lay down with the lion and everyone was happy. For some it was the hell on earth described by discharge, and that ought to be on the record.